caradise
ORIGINAL FLAVA™

CARIBBEAN COOKBOOK

BRING DA'FLAVA TO YOUR KITCHEN!

**Over 70 delicious, authentic & modern
Caribbean recipes made easy**

INCLUDING HEALTHIER INGREDIENT ALTERNATIVES

OUR STORY

We're two brothers, born and raised in London and we were taught how to cook authentic Caribbean food by our Grandma and Mum – who are Jamaican.

Growing up, we noticed that people loved Caribbean food but didn't know how to make it.

So, in April 2016, we created a Facebook page showing people how to make different Caribbean dishes in easy, one-minute videos.

One month later, we gained over 70,000 followers. And here we are today, with our first cookbook.

So here's our gift to you – easy-to-make authentic Caribbean recipes.

This book is dedicated to our Mum, Nanny Mitchell
& Nanny McAnuff (Rest in heavenly peace)

Caradise Original Flava
www.originalflava.com

First published by Craig McAnuff and Shaun McAnuff

Craig McAnuff and Shaun McAnuff asserts their moral right to be identified as the authors of this work.

Text © Craig McAnuff and Shaun McAnuff, 2017

Design © Craig Dean Studio

Photographs © AO Media 2017

Edited: Samantha Dennis

Stylist: Natalie Smith

Food styling: Craig Dean Studio

Food preparation: Shaun & Craig McAnuff

Printed and bound in Slovenia by Printing house KOPA

ISBN: 978-1-9998067-0-5

This book accompanies the content on originalflava.com

CONTENT

INTRODUCTION

Thank you for helping us bring da flava to your kitchen! Firstly, we want to dedicate this book to our Grandma and Mum for inspiring and teaching us how to cook from a young age – we wouldn't have started Original flava without them. And to everyone who contributed to making this book possible; this is for you too.

Wow! Is this real? We're really writing an introduction to our very own cookbook. So much has happened in just over a year. Who would have thought a small idea from two brothers in South London would have turned into an international platform, and now a cookbook? The truth is, the idea started organically. I was doing a project at university on Jamaican drinks and Shaun loved cooking at home. We both started reciting stories of how our colleagues would drool over the homecooked food we brought in for lunch. So we thought about making a page that showed them how to make it themselves; it was literally a lightbulb moment.

We then bought a camera and went to our grandma's house to shoot the videos – we wanted her approval on the recipes. Our first video got 1 million views in a week, followed by 70K+ online followers and TV interviews, all in the space of one month. We were in total shock! Now, one year and 300K followers, frontpage newspaper stories and more TV features later, we're here: with our first cookbook.

We're just two brothers from South London with a Jamaican background. We're passionate about Caribbean food and we want to share this with the world by showing how easy it is to make your favourite Caribbean dishes. And this is what our cookbook will help you to do.

Our aim is to bring da flava to your kitchen no matter your age or cultural background. This book will turn you into a Caribbean chef overnight. We have short online videos of some of the recipes – to make things even easier. Our recipes follow the motto E.A.T. which is, Easy to make; Accessible to purchase products and view our recipes online; and they're all tasty!

Caribbean food has become an increasingly popular choice for food lovers worldwide. However, it can be seen as a difficult cuisine to cook because of the various flavours. So we've broken it down for you. All you have to do is follow our recipes and you'll be making delicious Caribbean food in no time. Anyone can do it – including you. Yes, you!

We believe cooking is all about sharing and having fun. And with this, you're sure to have a great time. You can now spend less on take-away or eating out because you'll be too busy making your own food. And you'll have peace of mind because you know what's going into your dishes. It's a win win.

When we first started Original Flava, our main aim was to help people. We believe it's an important value to have in life and we've tried to implement this in business and our personal lives.

We want everybody to enjoy their food with friends and family. To know that you've made a delicious meal (from scratch) for yourself is priceless – and that moment should be shared. We grew up in a loving home with good values and we were always taught that it's better to give than to receive. And that's what we're doing with Original Flava. We're creating recipes and sharing them with people all over the world every week. And we're so grateful for the relationship we've built with our followers as a result.

This cookbook includes 70 of the best Caribbean recipes to keep you, your friends and family full and wanting more. We'd like to thank you for buying our cookbook. And to everyone that has supported us on this journey so far: you're a part of this cookbook and we couldn't have done this without you.

We hope you enjoy it.

Shaun & Craig

INGREDIENT LIST

Ackee

This is the national fruit of Jamaica and forms part of the national dish – Ackee and Saltfish. This unique fruit is usually eaten as a vegetable and you can buy it in a tin. Some people think Ackee is similar to scrambled eggs because of the look and texture.

All Purpose seasoning

This seasoning is used in the majority of Caribbean dishes. It's a mixture of different spices including pepper, salt, paprika, chilli, garlic and more.

Beans and Peas

Pigeon peas, kidney beans, black-eyed peas and yellow and green split peas are commonly used in Caribbean dishes. And beans are usually cooked with rice.

Breadfruit

Breadfruit is rich in starch, which transforms to sugars when very ripe. The fruits are roasted, baked, fried or boiled. When cooked, it's similar in taste to potatoes or baked bread.

Callaloo

Callaloo is a popular Caribbean vegetable and is similar to spinach. The dish originated in West Africa and is now served in different variants across the Caribbean. You can buy it fresh or in a tin.

Cho Cho

Jamaican cho cho is a tropical fruit that is a native of Mexico and Central America. They all have pear or slightly oval shapes. Cho Cho is a family of melons, gourds, squashes, and pumpkins and is mainly used in Caribbean soups or salads.

Coco bread

Coco bread is eaten in Jamaica and other areas of the Caribbean. The bread contains milk, flour and sugar and is starchy and sweet. It's mainly used as a sandwich and a Pattie is the filling.

Coconut

Coconut oil can be a healthier option for cooking oil – and it has a nice flavour.

Cornmeal

Cornmeal is a meal ground from dried maize. It's a common staple food, and is ground to fine, medium, and coarse consistencies. It's mainly used to make cornmeal porridge or cakes.

Curry powder

Curry powder is a mixture of turmeric, chilli powder, ground coriander, ground cumin. It's mainly used to make curry goat or curry chicken.

Escovitch

Escovitch is a traditional Jamaican dish for fish. It's when your fried fish is cooked with onions, peppers and carrots in vinegar.

Ginger

Ginger is one of the most ancient spices in worldwide cuisine. It's well-known for its health benefits. Caribbean's use it to make ginger beer and various curries.

Jerk

Jerk is a style of cooking where meat or fish is marinated with a variety of spices called Jamaican jerk spice.

Molasses

Molasses is a a sweetener that is formed as a byproduct of the sugar-making process and is used for a variety of sweets and cakes.

Oxtail

Oxtail is the culinary name for the tail of cattle. It is a very popular dish but can be expensive. It takes up to 3 hours to cook; it's very tender and is served with rice.

Plantain

The cousin of the banana, it's never eaten raw. It's not as starchy or sweet as a banana. It's commonly fried or boiled – or even made into fries.

Root vegetables

Root vegetables such as cassava, sweet potatoes, eddoes, dasheen and yams are mostly used in soups. They're hearty and nutritious.

Rice

Rice is a big part of Caribbean culture and is cooked regularly. It's served as rice and peas or cooked on it's own. Caribbean's typically use long grain or basmati rice.

Sweet potatoes

The sweet potato is a root vegetable, and is treated in a similar way to butternut squash, parsnips, swede and turnips.

Spring onion

Known in the Caribbean as Scallion. They're milder in taste to onions and are used in a lot of Caribbean recipes.

Saltfish

Saltfish is part of Jamaica's national dish. It must be soaked in water to remove the excess salt. It's best eaten with Ackee or Callaloo and served with dumplings or green banana. Frying Saltfish is the best way to prepare it.

Scotch bonnet

Scotch bonnet pepper is used in most Caribbean dishes. And it's very hot! Look for brightly-coloured chilies with no blemishes. If you prefer your food less spicy, remove the seeds from the chilli before cooking with it. Make sure you wash you hands after you handle them.

Seasoning meat

This is very important to Caribbean cuisine. To get the maximum flava from your food, it's best to season the meat correctly and marinate it for at least 2 hours – or overnight for even better results. Poke holes into the meat so that the seasoning can soak into the meat. Then, massage the seasoning into the meat vigourously. (Make sure you wash your hands thoroughly before and after.)

Tumeric

This spice is important to adding a yellow stain to food. It adds colour and flavour to many West Indian foods including curries and patties. (Caution: It will stain white and lightly-coloured clothes.)

Thyme

Thyme is an important herb for Caribbean cooking. It comes fresh on the sprigs, or dried. It gives a great flavour to many dishes and has many health benefits.

Washing meat

In caribbean culture, we were always taught to wash our meat before cooking. Lemons and limes are used in combination with vinegar to clean seafood, meat and poultry. They are added to the meat then rinsed thoroughly in water before before seasoning.

GINGER

OKRA

GREEN BANANA

SWEET POTATOES

PLANTAIN

SCOTCH BONNET

YAM

EARLY MAR'NING

Waking up in the morning to the sweet smell of breakfast was a time we looked forward to – and still do.
These recipes will hopefully bring you that same feeling so you can start your day in the best way: with some proper food!

Check out video recipes on originalflava.com

ACKEE & SALTFISH

The right place to start! It's Jamaica's national dish and one of our favourites. It's normally eaten in the morning but because of all the flavours, you'll probably want to eat it all day everyday. And most do – including us.

~~~~~~~~~~~~~~~~~

TIME: 30 MINS | SERVES: 6

INGREDIENTS

2 tbsp of vegetable oil*
2x 540g tins of ackee
2x 300g of boneless saltfish
1 medium green bell peppers *(chopped)*
1 medium tomato *(chopped)*
2 spring onion *(chopped)*
1 medium onion *(chopped)*
1 scotch bonnet
1 tsp of black pepper
1 tsp of all purpose seasoning
2 cloves of garlic finely chopped
Water *(enough to cover saltfish and boil)*

Optional:
Paprika
Tomato ketchup *(to reduce spice)*

DIRECTIONS

Boil the saltfish for 10 minutes and drain the water. Repeat this step twice. (Alternatively, soak the saltfish overnight in cold water, draining it and filling it with fresh water every 3 hours.)

Once saltfish is cool, tear and flake into small pieces and set aside.

Add 2 tablespoons of vegetable oil into medium heated frying pan. Then add chopped onions, green bell peppers, garlic, tomato, spring onion and scotch bonnet. Cook for 2 minutes.

Add the saltfish in the frying pan and dash some all purpose seasoning on it. Strain the liquid from the ackee down the sink and then add the ackee to the frying pan.

Dash a likkle bit of black pepper and stir gently. *(Be careful as the ackee will break – and nobody likes broken ackee!)* Simmer for 5 – 10 minutes and done!

FLAVA TIP
TRY WITH
~~~~~~~

Fried dumpling
Boiled dumpling
Green banana
Festival
Callaloo

Healthier Flava

*Olive oil or coconut oil

CORNMEAL PORRIDGE

We loved this porridge! Growing up, Grandma used to give this to us in the mornings. This sweet and smooth porridge will help to start your day off perfectly.

~~~~~~~

TIME: 45 MINUTES | SERVES: 4

INGREDIENTS

1 tsp of cinnamon
600ml whole milk
300g of fine yellow cornmeal
2 tbsp of sweet condensed milk*
1 tsp of nutmeg
A likkle bit of salt
Sugar to taste**
1 tsp of vanilla essence
950ml litre of water

DIRECTIONS

Mix together the cornmeal and whole milk into a bowl.

Pour the water into a pot and bring it to the boil on a high heat.

Add in the cornmeal and stir until the mixture thickens. Reduce to a medium heat once the mixture begins to bubble.

Mix in the cinnamon, sweet condensed milk, nutmeg, salt, sugar and vanilla.

Reduce to a low heat and let it simmer for 20 minutes. Allow cornmeal to rest for 10 minutes before serving.

PEANUT PORRIDGE

INGREDIENTS

1 tspn of cinnamon
250ml of coconut milk
1 tsp of nutmeg
250g of peanuts
200g of sweet condensed milk*
1 tsp of vanilla essence
125ml of water
2 tbsp of sugar**

DIRECTIONS

Blend peanuts and coconut milk together.

Then add water to a pot and let it boil.

Add the blended mixture to the water and stir.

Pour in the vanilla, sugar, cinnamon and nutmeg and continue stirring until the mixture thickens.

Add sweet condensed milk and then let it simmer for 20 minutes.

FLAVA TIP
TRY WITH
~~~~~~~
Hard dough bread

Healthier Flava
*soya/almond/lacto-free milk
**Put in some fruits to replace sugar

FRIED PLANTAIN

A Caribbean favourite: it's a delicious side dish to a variety of meals. It's best to fry it when the plantain is fairly ripe. So, that's when you can see some black spots on the skin. The darker the plantain, the sweeter it is.

TIME: 30 MINUTES | SERVES: 5

INGREDIENTS

2 ripe plantains
Vegetable oil* *(enough for shallow fry)*

DIRECTIONS

Using a sharp knife, cut off both tip ends and then gently score a line along the full length of plantain *(making sure you don't cut the inside flesh.)*

Remove the skin by peeling from the score line.

Put the plantain on a cutting board and cut it into slightly thick 45 degree angle pieces. On a high heat, add oil to the frying pan.

Once the oil is hot, lower it to a medium heat and then carefully place the plantain pieces to the pan. Let the pieces fry until they turn light brown on both sides.

Remove from frying pan, place on paper towel to drain excess oil.

FLAVA TIP
TRY WITH

Ackee and saltfish

Healthier Flava

Rapeseed oil

Local FOOD

THORNTON HEATH, SOUTH LONDON

OUT OF MANY THE WORLD'S X FASTEST PEOPLE

MACKEREL RUNDOWN

A very filling, traditional Jamaican breakfast of well-seasoned mackerel cooked in coconut milk *(tinned or fresh)*, served with 'hard food' – boiled dumplings and green banana. Start your day off right with this dish. Ah propa yard food dis!

~~~~~~~~~~~~~~~~~~~~~~~~

TIME: 1 HOUR | SERVES: 3-4

INGREDIENTS

1 large fresh mackerel *(cut into pieces)* or 400g tinned mackarel

2 green bananas

1 tsp of sugar

250g plain flour

Water

1 x can 400ml coconut milk

¼ medium red bell peppers *(sliced)*

¼ medium green bell peppers *(sliced)*

¼ medium yellow bell peppers *(sliced)*

1 medium onion *(chopped)*

1 medium tomato *(chopped)*

4 cloves garlic *(finely chopped)*

3 spring onions *(chopped)*

1 tbsp of curry powder

1 tsp of fish seasoning

1 tsp of all purpose seasoning

1 whole scotch bonnet pepper

DIRECTIONS

Fresh mackerel process

Remove the bones from the mackerel and cut into 2-3 inch pieces. Place in a heatproof bowl.

Pour boiling water over fish until covered and soak for 30 minutes. Drain water and set fish aside.

Pour coconut milk into saucepan and bring to boil over medium-high heat. Stir until it reduces to a thick custard consistency with oil visible on top.

Add curry powder, onion, bell peppers, garlic, tomato, spring onions, fish seasoning, and scotch bonnet pepper and then stir. Sauté everything until onions are transparent.

Add fish to pan *(if using tinned mackerel, add in here)*, skin-side down, and spoon the sauce over the fish. Reduce to a low heat and simmer for about 10 minutes until the fish is cooked.

Green banana

Cut off tips on both ends, and score the full length of the green banana. Then place in boiling salted water for 20 minutes. *(Add ½ tsp of salt)*

Once finished, take out bananas with tongs, and peel off the skin.

For boiled dumplings directions see page 36.

VEGETABLE RUNDOWN

A vegetarian spin on the mackerel rundown. Start your day off right with this filling breakfast.

~~~~~~~~~~~~~~~~

TIME: 1 HOUR | SERVES: 5

INGREDIENTS

1 tsp of all purpose seasoning
½ a medium broccoli *(sliced)*
1 tbsp of butter
2 medium carrots *(sliced)*
1 x 400ml tin of coconut milk
¼ cup of callaloo or spinach
1 medium onion *(sliced)*
3 spring onions *(chopped)*
1 tsp of black pepper
¼ medium red bell peppers *(sliced)*
¼ medium green bell peppers *(sliced)*
¼ medium yellow bell peppers *(sliced)*
1 scotch bonnet pepper *(chopped)*
A likkle bit of salt
4 sprigs of fresh thyme

DIRECTIONS

Melt your butter in a frying pan on a high heat. Sauté the onion, spring onions, and fresh thyme for 2 minutes.

Add the carrots, bell peppers and broccoli and cook for another 2 minutes. Pour in the coconut milk and cook until it thickens. *(Put a lid on the pan to help thicken the sauce.)*

Add callaloo, black pepper, salt, all purpose seasoning and mix together. Then let it simmer on a low-medium heat for 5 minutes.

CARIBBEAN / ENGLISH BREAKFAST

Growing up in London and living with a Caribbean family meant
we often mixed breakfasts from both cultures. You can't go
wrong with the best of both! Ackee & saltfish, fried dumplings,
plantain, sausages, baked beans, hard dough bread.

~~~~~~~~

TIME: 1 HOUR 15 MINS | SERVES: 2-4

INGREDIENTS

1 x 540g tin of ackee
1 tsp of all purpose seasoning
4 rashers of smoked bacon
1 x 400g tin of baked beans
2 green banana
2 slices of hardough bread
Water
450g self-raising flour
2 cloves of garlic (chopped)
2 medium onions (chopped)
1 tsp of paprika
2 ripe plantains
1 tsp of black pepper
1 scotch bonnet pepper (chopped)
1 tsp of salt
300g of saltfish
4 sausages
200g of tomatoes (chopped)
1 tsp of sugar
1 tsp of dried thyme
2 tbsp of vegetable oil

DIRECTIONS

For *ackee and salt fish* directions, see page 14

Seasoned baked beans process:

In a separate pan, add some vegetable oil, garlic and onions
and fry for 2 minutes.

Add your baked beans and season with onions, black pepper and
thyme. Let it simmer for 5 minutes.

Bacon & sausages process:

In a separate frying pan, turn on medium heat and fry the bacon
and sausages in vegetable oil until cooked.

Green banana process:

Cut off tips on both ends, and score the full length of the green
banana. Then place in boiling salted water for 20 minutes.
(½ tsp of salt)

Once finished, take out bananas with tongs, and peel off the skin.

For *fried plantain* directions, see page 19.

Serve with a slice of hard dough bread and nyam!

MANGO & BANANA SMOOTHIE

There's no smoothie like a Caribbean smoothie – especially these fruit flavas. This recipe will leave you feeling like you're in the Caribbean.

~~~~~~~~~~

INGREDIENTS

1 chopped banana
150ml of coconut milk or
fat-free milk
1 tablespoon of honey
5 cup of ice
1 medium lime *(squeezed)*
1 medium mango ripe, peeled
and cubed

DIRECTIONS

Put all the ingredients into the blender – including the ice – and blend until it's smooth.

Test it with a spoon to see if the consistency is right.

SERVES: 2

TASTE OF THE CARIBBEAN

INGREDIENTS

1 medium mango ripe, peeled
and cubed
5 ice cubes
2 passion fruits flesh scooped out
or 200ml passion fruit juice
½ a medium banana
250ml orange juice.

DIRECTIONS

Put all the ingredients into the blender – including the ice – and blend until it's smooth.

Test it with a spoon to see if the consistency is right.

SERVES: 2

FLAVA TIP

Fruits can be fresh or frozen.

MAR'NIN BOOST!

You know those morning when you need that lift? This one will do the trick. It's full of natural sugars from the fruit so it'll give you the energy you need to g'yet up 'n go!

INGREDIENTS

½ an apple
1 medium banana
½ a pear
125g of strawberries
½ a cup of water
Handful of ice

DIRECTIONS

Put all the ingredients into a blender and blend until smooth.

~~~~~~~~~~~~~~~~~

TIME: 5 MINS | SERVES: 4

GREEN FLAVA

This drink acts as a flavasome antioxidant and is full of vitamins A,C and E. It's also packed with protein and minerals to help with digestion, and is high in fibre - so your skin can look younger. Yah man!

INGREDIENTS

1 green apple
½ an avocado
A handful of ice cubes
1 kiwi (peeled)
30g of spinach
125ml of water

DIRECTIONS

Put all the ingredients into a blender and blend until smooth.

~~~~~~~~~~~~~~~~~

TIME: 5 MINS | SERVES: 4

FLAVA TIP

Fruits can be fresh or frozen.

PON DI SIDE

Caribbean food is famously know for the flavalicious side dishes. They are the perfect complements for mains, and are just as great on their own.

RICE & PEAS

This dish is one of the most popular Jamaican dishes. Its seasoned rice and soft peas complements any meat dish. We used to have this at home every Sunday and then on Monday leftovers. (I'm sure we weren't the only ones.) Give it a go: rice and peas made easy!

~~~~~~~~~~~~~~~~~

TIME: 1 HOURS 45 MINS | SERVES: 4-6

INGREDIENTS

400g dry or canned gungo peas or kidney beans

1 medium onion *(chopped)*

2 spring onions *(chopped in half)*

4 sprigs of thyme

1 whole scotch bonnet pepper

1 tsp of black pepper

1 tsp of salt

2 cloves garlic *(chopped)*

400ml coconut milk or 60g of creamed coconut

600g of rice* *(long grain or basmati)*

1 tbsp of all purpose seasoning
Water

Optional:
Butter

1 tsp pimento seeds or all spice *(for extra spice!)*

DIRECTIONS

Dry peas process

Pour dry red kidney beans or gungo peas in a large pot, pour in water *(5 cm above the peas)* and soak overnight.

Canned peas process

Pour canned red kidney beans or gungo peas *(including liquid in can)* in a large pot, add water *(5 cm above the peas)* and soak overnight.

Place the pot on the stove, add salt, black pepper, onions, fresh thyme, spring onions, chopped garlic, all purpose seasoning, coconut milk or creamed coconut. If using dry peas, boil for around 1 hour, until the peas are soft. If using canned peas, just bring to a boil. *Add more water if neccessary.*

Wash the rice thoroughly and pour into pot. Make sure water is level just above rice. Mix together, add scotch bonnet pepper and place lid on top of pot. Then cook for 25-30 mins on medium-low heat.

Take out scotch bonnet pepper and mix rice thoroughly from the bottom.

Healthier Flava

*Brown rice

TRY WITH

Jerk Chicken
Curry goat
Oxtail
Fried coconut chicken

FLAVA TIP

- Cover the rice with foil and place the lid on top, this will help it to cook quicker.

- Dry peas take longer to cook than canned peas.

MACARONI & CHEESE PIE

Cheeeeze! If you're a cheese lover you will adore this one! It combines 4 different cheeses, is well-seasoned and has a crunchy topping.

~~~~~~

Time: 50 MINUTES | Serves: 10-12

INGREDIENTS

1 tbsp of butter
1 tsp of chilli powder
2 beaten eggs
450ml evaporated milk or whole milk
50g of flour
200g of four cheese
1kg of macaroni
200g of mature cheese
200g of mild cheddar
200g of mozzarella
1 tsp of mustard
½ a small onion *(diced)*
1 tsp of paprika
1 tsp of black pepper
A likkle bit of salt
1 scotch bonnet pepper *(chopped)*
Water

Optional:
Cheese crackers (It helps to give extra crunch)

FLAVA TIP
Great for family events & BBQ's

DIRECTIONS

Add water and salt to a pan, bring to the boil and then add the macaroni. *(Cook for 10 minutes.)*

Pour evaporated or whole milk to a mixing bowl and mix together with eggs, flour, mustard, paprika, chilli powder, black pepper, scotch bonnet pepper and the onion.

Drain the macaroni and place into a mixing bowl. Add butter and 50g of each mature, mild and mozzarella cheese and mix into the pasta.

Pour the liquid mix onto the pasta and stir.

Spoon a thin layer of macaroni into a deep oven dish and then sprinkle mild cheddar over it.

Add another layer of macaroni and then sprinkle mature cheddar over it. *(Repeat these steps until you've used all the pasta.)*

Then line the top with the four cheeses and bake for 30 minutes at 180 degrees heat.

If you want, you can add crushed cheese crackers on top to give it an extra crunch.

FRIED DUMPLING

One of the caribbeans most drool-worthy snacks! It's a sweet bread that'll turn your 'I'll only have one' into, 'Yup, I'm going for my seventh!' With a crunchy exterior and soft core, there's no taste like it!

~~~~~~~~~~

TIME: 20 MINUTES | SERVES: 5-6

INGREDIENTS

500g of self-raising flour
A likkle bit of sugar
Water
Vegetable oil *(enough to shallow fry)*

Optional added Flava:
Milk
½ tbsp of butter
A likkle bit of salt
1 tsp of baking powder
(if you're using plain flour)

Healthier Flava

**Gluten-free flour
Use less vegetable oil
Remove sugar, butter and salt*

DIRECTIONS

Dough process:

Add flour into a mixing bowl, then add a likkle bit of sugar and mix with your hands.

Then add small amounts of water, kneading it in with your hands. Continue until you have a large ball of dough. *(If your dough is dry, add a likkle more water and knead it into the dough. And if it's too wet, dash in some flour.)*

Tear off a small piece of dough to begin making your dumplings and place it in the palm of one hand. Then move the dough around in a circular motion with your other palm. Once a ball shape is created, gently press the ball down a likkle.

Frying process:

Generously pour vegetable oil enough for a shallow fry into a frying pan and place onto a medium/high heat.

Fry the dumplings on either side until golden brown.

Place a paper towel on a plate and then place the fried dumplings onto it to soak up the excess oil.

BOILED DUMPLINGS

Mix everything together making sure the dough is very firm. *(It shouldn't be the same consistency as the dough for fried dumplings otherwise it'll lose it's shape when you boil it.)*

Half-fill a deep and wide pot with water and bring it to the boil Place the dumplings in the pot and let it boil for 20 minutes.

Put a pot lid over the dumplings but don't cover it completely. If you do, the water will spill out.

Lower the fire slightly and leave to boil for another 15 minutes.

Pierce a fork into one of the dumplings to test if it's ready. It should be firm all the way through.

FLAVA TIP
TRY WITH

~~~~

*Escovitch fish
Ackee & salt fish
Green banana
Seasoned beans*

FESTIVAL

AKA the dumplings' older brother. Festival has a similar texture but it's crunchier and richer in flavour. A great on-the-go snack, ideal for any time of the day – and it's delicious!

~~~~~~~~~~~~~~~~~~~

TIME: 30 MINUTES | SERVES: 6

INGREDIENTS

3 tsp of baking powder
250g fine cornmeal
450g of flour*
Vegetable oil *(enough to shallow fry)*
1 tsp of salt
3 tsp of sugar
A likkle bit of salt
1 tsp of vanilla
Water

DIRECTIONS

Put the cornmeal and flour into a bowl and mix it together.

Add the baking powder, salt, sugar and vanilla to the cornmeal and flour, then mix together.

Pour in the water and mix with your hands. Work in the rest of the water gradually, and continue to bring the mixture together until it forms a large ball.

Place the dough in foil and leave it in the fridge for 30 minutes.

Cut the dough into 8 pieces and carefully roll into long, thick sausage shapes *(like in our picture)*.

Put 1 cup of oil into a frying pan and make sure it's on a high heat. The oil should be hot – but not piping hot – before you add the dough. *(If the oil's giving off smoke, it's too hot.)*

Place a few festivals into the pan and cook until it's golden brown on both sides.

Put the festivals on a paper towel to soak up the excess oil.

FLAVA TIP
TRY WITH

~~~~~~~~~

Escovitch fish
Curry goat
Jerk chicken

Healthier Flava
*Gluten-free flour
Use less vegetable oil
Remove sugar, butter and salt

VEGETABLE CURRY NOODLES

This is an E.A.T recipe: easy, accessible and tasty! It's a quick and simple meal. So if you like a bit of spice in your life, this one's for you.

~~~

TIME: 10 MINUTES | SERVES: 2-3

INGREDIENTS

4 tbsp of curry powder

3 cloves of garlic

Likkle bit of salt

1 tsp of black pepper

1 tsp of ginger

¼ of an onion *(sliced)*

1 tsp of paprika

1 scotch bonnet pepper *(sliced – remove seeds)*

400g of fresh egg noodles

2 spring onions *(sliced)*

1 tbsp of vegetable oil*

DIRECTIONS

Add the vegetable oil to a frying pan and place on a high heat.

Fry the onions, scotch bonnet pepper, ginger, garlic, spring onions and cook for 3 minutes on medium heat.

Add the curry powder, salt, black pepper and paprika and stir in.

Separate the noodles and then add them to the pan with a few pinches of curry powder.

Mix together and let it simmer for 2-3 minutes.

Healthier Flava
Coconut or rapeseed oil

COCONUT RICE

TIME: 10 MINUTES | SERVES: 2-3

~~~

INGREDIENTS

500g basmati rice

125ml of coconut milk or 60g block coconut crème

1 tsp of butter

Water *(water should be level with the rice)*

1 tsp of salt

DIRECTIONS

Firstly wash rice 3-4 time

Then place rice into a pot, and level water with rice.

Then pour coconut milk into the pot and mix gently.

Add salt, butter and stir.

Leave on medium heat for 15 minutes max.

Then use a folk to fold and mix the rice from the base of pot.

Then serve.

MEET SHAUN

I've always enjoyed cooking. Growing up in a Caribbean household meant cooking was a massive part of my life. My Mum and Grandma were always in the kitchen cooking for the family. In those days, women were known to be in the kitchens while the husband was the breadwinner, which is why I always remembered my dad being at work and my mum cooking. The only time my mum rested was on a Friday – takeaway day – otherwise I would help with the cooking, or I'd go in to the kitchen to check when dinner was ready. And that's how it was at my grandma's too – not that I'm complaining.

Having grown up around Caribbean food, I got used to the sweet-smelling recipes that woke me out of my sleep. Things like Ackee and Saltfish in the morning and the smell of Rice and Peas on a Sunday. Easter time was my favourite. My grandma would make Fried Fish and there was always plenty of Carrot juice – it was delicious. And how could I forget about Christmas? We had so much food and drinks. Sorrel and Guinness punch filled the fridge. I wanted to know how to make everything, so over the years, I learned from my Mum and Grandma. Luckily, the recipes stuck with me. So when I had to fend for myself at uni, I never went hungry.

I grew up in a loving home. My Mum and Dad are Christians and we all attended church regularly growing up. I always remember them serving patties and ginger beer once church had finished. I really looked forward to that!

As I got older, I went to college and then university. I studied Art and Design Media and computers. But throughout my education, I never really knew what I wanted to do with my life. I'd say I had an indecisive personality, which meant making big decisions in life was always a struggle for me. I went from wanting to be an artist, to a graphic designer and then an event manager and, get this, a nurse. (Yes, I know, random!) I had a number of customer-focused jobs because I enjoyed helping people. I then started to work with young people with learning difficulties, helping them to live independently in the future and I really enjoyed that. I would do cooking sessions with them every week, teaching them how to make the Caribbean food my mum and grandma had taught me. And once I did that, I thought I'd found my destiny.

A few months down the line, the company had to let me go and I was gutted. So I went back to customer service and was back to not knowing what I wanted to do with my life. The only thing I knew was that I loved cooking and it made me really happy, but I didn't see it as anything more. I remember cooking for family and friends and I would cook if my mum was at work because my dad couldn't cook to save his life. I remember there was a time when he burned our oven chips – so my mum did the cooking after that. I also used to cook for one of my girlfriends all the time – she was very lucky – and I went as far as making her packed lunches. (I must've been in love.)

I'd take my food in to work for lunch as my grandma always told me not to take in takeaway food. So I tried my hardest not to. And to be honest, I preferred cooking for myself anyway; I'd choose Jerk chicken over a normal burger any day. So, on Mondays I would bring in the leftovers from Sunday nights' dinner: Rice and peas and jerk chicken, and a variety of dishes throughout the week. My work colleagues started to notice the different aromas coming from the work canteen and would purposely come in to see what food I was eating. They always complimented the food. One of my colleagues, who had travelled quite a bit to the Caribbean was familiar with the smell of Caribbean food. Whenever he came into the canteen he would say, in a fake Jamaican accent, 'what food you ah eat today?', and I would laugh. He asked if I knew how to make the food I was eating, and my reply was always yes. He was so surprised and wanted to know who had taught me. Then he said he'd love to know how to make Caribbean food so that he doesn't have to rely on Caribbean restaurants.

Later that day, I spoke to Craig about what had been happening and he said he was getting the same reaction from his work colleagues. And as Craig had an idea for a project at uni regarding Jamaican drinks that he wanted to develop, we started brainstorming ways we could bring Caribbean food to people. Then we thought about showing people how to make authentic Caribbean food online. One thing led to another and then we had 70K followers in the first month! It all happened so quickly. I'm still a bit shocked but I'm grateful for all the support and I'm loving the journey. It's also brought Craig and I closer together as brothers, which is great!

Shaun's
Favourite Dish

CARIBBEAN FRIED RICE

When Caribbean meets Chinese-style rice. It's our spicy rice with tender chicken and assorted vegetables. Save a bit of cash and have this on takeaway night instead. It'll taste better because you made it yourself!

~~~~~~~~~~~

TIME: 50 MINS | SERVES: 4-6

INGREDIENTS

1 tsp of all purpose seasoning
1 tbsp of butter
150g of carrots (diced)
300g of chicken breast
3 cloves of garlic (chopped)
1 tsp of grated ginger
½ medium onion (diced)
2 spring onions (chopped)
1 tsp of paprika
100g of garden peas
1 tsp of black pepper
1 scotch bonnet pepper (chopped)
250g of white rice**
A likkle bit of salt
2 tbsp of soy sauce
100g of sweetcorn
1 tsp of dried thyme
150g of stir fry vegetables
2 tbsp of vegetable oil*

DIRECTIONS

Wash your rice and add to pot, levelling water just above rice. Cook for 20 minutes.

Dice your chicken breast into small pieces and season with black pepper, all purpose, paprika and a likkle bit of salt.

Add vegetable oil to a frying pan and place on a high heat. Turn down to medium heat, then sauté the garlic, onions and scotch bonnet pepper.

Add the chicken and fry until golden brown.

Mix in the spring onions, sweetcorn, garden peas, stir fry vegetables, carrots and ginger.

Add the cooked rice to the frying pan with soy sauce and butter – stir until all ingredients are mixed into the rice.

Simmer for 10 minutes on a low heat.

Healthier Flava
*Coconut oil, rapeseed oil, or olive oil
**Brown rice or quinoa

CALLALOO AND SALTFISH

If you haven't tasted callaloo before, it's like a mixture of kale and spinach. It complements saltfish, which makes it a flavasome side dish. *(Traditionally, though, it includes bacon – but that's optional.)*

~~~~~~~~~~

TIME: 30 MINUTES | SERVES: 2-4

INGREDIENTS

1 tsp of all purpose seasoning
1 x 540g tin of callaloo
4 cloves of garlic *(chopped)*
1 medium onion *(sliced)*
1 medium red onion *(sliced)*
2 spring onions *(chopped)*
1 tsp of paprika
1 tsp of black pepper
½ medium red bell pepper *(diced)*
1 scotch bonnet pepper *(diced)*
300g of saltfish
1 teaspoon of vegetable oil*

DIRECTIONS

Boil the saltfish for 10 minutes and drain the water. Repeat this step twice. (Alternatively, soak the saltfish overnight in cold water, draining it and filling it with fresh water every 3 hours.)

Put a pan on a high heat and add vegetable oil. Then fry the garlic, onions, scotch bonnet pepper and spring onions.

Add the saltfish, callaloo and mix in. Then add the black pepper, paprika and all purpose and let it simmer for 4-5 minutes.

FLAVA TIP
TRY WITH
~~~~

Bacon
Fried or boiled dumpling
Boiled green banana
Fried plantain

Healthier Flava
*Coconut oil, rapeseed oil or olive oil

CARIBBEAN COLESLAW

We used to love going to our Aunty Janet's house growing up because she made the most incredible coleslaw! So we got the recipe and added out likkle twist. We love it so much, we could eat it on it's own.

~~~~~~

TIME: 30 MINUTES | SERVES: 6

INGREDIENTS

½ a medium white cabbage

2 carrots

5 tbsp of mayonnaise

1 medium onion *(sliced)*

1 tsp of black pepper

¼ medium green bell pepper *(diced)*

¼ medium red bell pepper *(diced)*

1 tbsp of salad cream

A likkle bit of salt

½ a scotch bonnet pepper or
1 tbsp of hot pepper sauce

165g of sweetcorn

DIRECTIONS

Finely grate your carrots and cabbage in a large bowl and mix together.

Dice the onion and add sweetcorn in the bowl and mix together.

Then dice the green and red peppers and the scotch bonnet pepper *(remove seeds)* then add to the bowl.

Add the mayonnaise, salad cream, salt and black pepper and mix together.

FLAVA TIP
TRY WITH
~~~~~~

Jerk Chicken
Rice and peas
Great for BBQ's

PEPPER PRAWNS

Spicy flavours combined with the subtle shell crunch and soft inner flesh, this can be used as a delicious starter to serve during dinner parties or 3 course meal.

~~~~~~~~~

TIME: 15 MINUTES | SERVES: 5

INGREDIENTS

1lb raw shelled shrimp
¼ onions *(diced)*
3 cloves garlic *(finely chopped)*
2 scotch bonnet pepper *(chopped – add more scotch bonnet if ya bad!)*
1 tsp black pepper
1 tsp all purpose seasoning
1 tsp paprika
½ cup parsley *(finely chopped)*
2 tbsp vegetable oil
1 tbsp lemon juice
Lime

DIRECTIONS

Add 1 tablespoon vegetable oil to the frying pan on high heat.

Turn to medium heat. Then add onions, garlic, and scotch bonnet and cook for 2 mins.

Wash shrimp with lime and water. Trim legs and antenna (optional). Add shrimp to the pan and stir and cook for 2-3 mins.

Add black pepper, all purpose seasoning, and paprika. Stir and cook for further 2-3 mins.

Add ½ cup of parsley and 1 tablespoon of lemon juice and simmer for 2 mins.

FLAVA TIP
Wash your hands, after touching scotch bonnet

Healthier Flava
Coconut oil

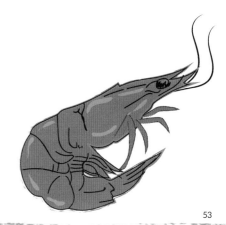

STIR-FRY PLANTAIN AND PRAWN

One word for this dish – delicious. And it only takes 30 minutes to make. A wonderful mixture of spice and sweetness. You can have this healthy dish for lunch or dinner whether you're at home or on-the-go.

~~~~~

TIME: 30 MINUTES | SERVES: 2-4

INGREDIENTS

1 tsp all purpose seasoning
1 tsp black pepper
Likkle bit of Himalayan salt
Lemon
2 tsp of thyme
2 tbsp coconut oil
1 tbsp of honey
1 large onion *(diced)*
2 plantains
150g of uncooked prawns
A likkle bit of sea salt
2 spring onions *(chopped)*
1 scotch bonnet pepper *(chopped)*
2 tsp thyme

For dressing (optional)
Sweet chilli sauce

DIRECTIONS

For the Plantain:

Slice the plantain so that it's half an inch thick and put into a bowl.

Season with 1 teaspoon of all purpose, black pepper, Himalayan salt and 1 tsp thyme.

Pour the coconut oil into a frying pan and place on a medium heat.

Once the oil is hot, fry the plantain on each side for 3-4 minutes until it's golden brown.

(Place onto a paper towel to drain off the excess oil.)

For the prawns:

Wash the prawns with water and lemon.

Season with 1 teaspoon of thyme, all purpose, Himalayan salt and mix together.

On a medium heat, spray coconut oil into the pan and fry the onions, scotch bonnet and spring onions for 5 minutes.

Add the prawns and stir. Then add the scotch bonnet pepper and honey and cook for 5 minutes.

MEET CRAIG

I couldn't have asked for a better upbringing. I had a supportive family around me and a good set of bruddahs (friends) close by. Despite that, I found myself in challenging situations.

Growing up in Thornton Heath, South London, everyone knew everyone. No one was a stranger to gang affiliation, including me. I was a part of a few gangs – I say gangs, but really, it was just a group of friends and people I was cool with. We weren't involved in mass murders or drug smuggling from certain countries. However, there were a few instances that shaped me into the man I am today.

The experience that sticks out the most – like a Michelin star restaurant on Thornton Heath high street – was when I came face-to-face with a gun on the bus. I was 14 years old and some boys came up to the top deck of the bus and walked towards the back were I sat with my friends. They asked us lots of questions – or "moving to us" as we used to say – and I cheekily replied, 'why so many questions? Is this who wants to be

a millionaire?' The boy was so vexed, he flipped, which made me laugh.
He then, in his anger, said, 'you think you're bad?', and then approached
me, fumbled for something in the front of his trousers and revealed a
gun. Surprisingly, I wasn't scared at all. I thought it was a fake and, in my
'tough man conscience', I thought I was untouchable.
So I continued laughing and he tightened his grip around the gun and
got angrier. My friend, Mark, who was sitting beside me was even crazier
than I was. He started shouting, 'go on, then. Shoot us. Shoot me right
here in the head.' Looking back I can see how absolutely crazy Mark and
me were, but at the time it happened, I had no fear.

We continued the feud off the bus and I was still under the impression
that the gun was fake. When we got off the bus, the boy with the gun
shouted, 'what you saying?', and I responded, 'what are you saying?
You approached me with a gun.' And that's when he told me it was
because I 'got rude'. To my amazement, I found myself saying, 'I don't
have time for this, I'm a child of God,' and I walked away. And in that
moment, the world stood still and I expected bullet holes in my back that
would ultimately send me to meet my maker. But nothing happened.
My boys walked beside me and we continued our day as if nothing
had happened.

The next day, a friend of mine who knew the gunman, told me it was a real gun and that he'd got it for protection from some boys that were after him that week. I was dumbfounded. That moment made me realise I could have been dead. I don't know why I said I was a child of God to him because I was ashamed to be a believer growing up. I grew up in a Christian home, though, so maybe it was fear or being scared of what could happen next that gripped my heart. Who knows?

I've seen many young guys getting pulled into street crime. Pride and the desire to be respected was my Achilles heel. Others might be different, but I know some young people do struggle with that same thing, however I truly believe there's a way out for those who really want to succeed in life.

Looking back, that was a pivotal point in my life. I wasn't doing well in school, and was predicted failures in my exams by my teachers. I saw other young guys either dying, going to prison or going down that path. I didn't want my parents to get a visit from the police, I wanted to make them – and my future family – proud of me and my journey. They were the reason I turned my life around. So I knuckled down and went on to get a degree, and now I wear many hats; I'm the director of 2 business, Craig Dean studio, where I'm a creative director and a graphic designer – not to mention, a food fanatic and co-owning Original Flava with my brother Shaun.

I can only thank God, friends and family for helping me to not become another statistic. To any young person struggling to find inspiration to succeed in life, find your reason. Whether it's making your parents proud, proving someone wrong who didn't believe in you, or it's to leave a legacy for your kids, let it be your main motivation. Where there's a will there's a way.

Craig's
Favourite Dish
Escovitch Fish

PLANTAIN FRIES

Trust me on this: this is just as good as french fries *(or chips for my British folks.)* We were fighting over who had the last chip on the plate - that's how good they were! Give it a try.

TIME: 15 MINUTES | SERVES: 2-3

INGREDIENTS

200ml of coconut milk*
2 tbsp of cornflour
2 tbsp of plain flour**
2 plantain
2 cups of vegetable oil
120ml of water
1 tbsp of vegetable oil

DIRECTIONS

Slice the plantain into chips and put into a bowl.

Season with plain flour, corn flour, coconut milk and water and mix together.

Pour the vegetable oil in a frying pan on a high heat.

Add the chips (one at a time) and fry until golden brown.

Place onto a paper towel to drain off the excess oil.

FLAVA TIP
TRY WITH

Dirty jerk burger

Healthier Flava

*Coconut oil, rapeseed oil or olive oil
** Gluten-free flour
***Bake in oven instead of frying

ROAST BREADFRUIT

Authentic caribbean food at it's finest. It's high in protein and similar in taste to baked potato. You can grill, bake or fry it.

~~~~~~

TIME: 1 HOUR 20 MINUTES | SERVES: 5

INGREDIENTS

1 medium size breadfruit
2 tbsp of vegetable oil*
A likkle salt

DIRECTIONS

Grill the breadfruit, or place in a oven for 1 hour until it turns black.

Leave it to cool and then peel off the skin. Remove the seed in the middle and cut the breadfruit into small pieces.

On a medium heat, add vegetable oil to a frying pan and fry the breadfruit on each side until golden brown. *(Or you can bake it in the oven until golden brown.)*

Let it rest on paper towel to drain oil.

Sprinkle a likkle salt on it and nyam! (eat)

FLAVA TIP
TRY WITH
~~~~~~

Mackerel rundown
Escovitch fish
Ackee & saltfish

Healthier Flava
*Coconut oil

BAMMY

A traditional Jamaican cassava flat bread. Usually eaten with Fried fish, it can be toasted or baked and provides a crispy crunch when eaten.

TIME: 25 MINUTES | SERVES: 2-4

INGREDIENTS

397g pack of bammy
Vegetable oil* (enough to shallow fry)
225ml coconut milk

DIRECTIONS

Soak Bammy in coconut milk and let it sit for 15 mins. Then cut Bammy into 4 quarters.

Add vegetable oil into a frying pan on high heat. Then add Bammy quarters to pan and fry for 6 minutes on each side until golden brown.

Then rest Bammy on paper towel to remove excess oil.

FLAVA TIP
TRY WITH

Mackerel rundown
Escovitch fish
Stir fry cabbage

Healthier Flava

*Coconut oil

STIR FRY CABBAGE

Cabbage is the main feature of this dish, however it's filled with other crunchy caribbean assorted vegetables. It tastes great, it's colourful and it's healthy. What more could you want from this side dish?

TIME: 25 MINUTES | SERVES: 4

INGREDIENTS

¼ medium white cabbage *(sliced)*
1 cup peel carrots *(sliced)*
1 medium onion *(sliced)*
2 spring onions *(sliced)*
¼ medium red bell pepper *(sliced)*
¼ medium green bell pepper *(sliced)*
¼ medium yellow bell pepper *(sliced)*
1 tsp of black pepper
1 tsp of salt
2 tbsp of vegetable oil*
1 tsp of thyme
1 tbsp of butter**

DIRECTIONS

On a high heat, pour vegetable oil into a frying pan.

Turn down to medium heat and add carrots, cabbage, onion, spring onions, and bell peppers. Mix together while it's cooking. Dash black pepper, salt, thyme, butter and simmer for 15 mins.

FLAVA TIP
TRY WITH

Dairy free butter

Healthier Flava
*Coconut oil, rapeseed oil or olive oil
**Dairy-free butter

CARNIVAL STREET FOOD

Carrnnivall! The ultimate party atmosphere, popular for its caribbean cultural influence and food. The next section provides the most popular snacks and drinks taken from the biggest event in the world!

▶ Check out video recipes on originalflava.com

JERK CHICKEN

There's no chicken like jerk chicken! Succulent grilled pieces of marinated chicken with a crispy coating – there's no summer bbq without it! Applied with our BBQ Jerk sauce – it's flavalicious!

INGREDIENTS

8 chicken leg quarters
4 tbsp of jerk paste
Jerk BBQ sauce
1 tbsp of jerk seasoning

FLAVA TIP
TRY WITH

Rice & peas
Macaroni cheese

DIRECTIONS

Wash chicken with lemon and water and pat dry.

Poke holes in chicken with a knife, put in a large bowl and add jerk seasoning and jerk paste. Massage into chicken and then marinate in the fridge overnight.

Pre-heat your charcoal bbq grill and place chicken on grill at medium heat and cook until chicken is brown and slightly crispy on both sides. *(Check temperature of meat is at least 165 degrees.)*

Glaze bbq jerk sauce on the chicken and rest on cooler parts of the grill, close grill and cook for 10 minutes.

Chicken done. Now enjoy & EAT di ting!

JERK MARINADE

INGREDIENTS

2 tsp of allspice
4 tbsp of brown sugar
1 tsp of browning or soy sauce
1 tsp of cinnamon
4 cloves of garlic
1 tsp of nutmeg
1 medium onion *(chopped)*
1 tsp of black pepper
2 scotch bonnet peppers
2 spring onion *(chopped)*
1 tsp of dried thyme
60ml of vinegar
Squeeze of lime juice

DIRECTIONS

Blend all these ingredients in blender until smooth.

Massage onto meat and marinate in fridge overnight.

Notting Hill
CARNIVAL
LONDON

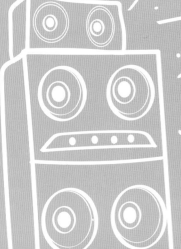

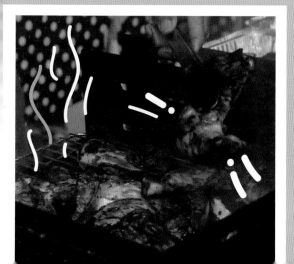

The biggest street event in Europe! We love it here,

Great **VIBES,**
FOOD AND PEOPLE

JERK PORK

One of Jamaica's signature bbq dishes. The juicy flavas of jerk pork on a summer's day grilled to perfection is guaranteed to have the family and friends jerking for joy!

~~~~~~~~~~~~~

TIME: 1 HOUR | SERVES: 6

INGREDIENTS

1.7kg large pork belly/shoulder/joint

2 tbsp of jerk seasoning

Jerk bbq sauce

Lemon

4 tbsp of jerk marinade/paste *(or make your own jerk marinade, see recipe on page 71)*

DIRECTIONS

Wash pork with lemon and water and pat dry.

Put pork joint in a large bowl, pierce meat with a knife and season with jerk paste and jerk seasoning. Massage it into the pork and then marinate in the fridge overnight.

Pre-heat your charcoal bbq grill and place pork on grill at medium heat. Cook until pork is brown and crispy on both sides. *(Check temperature of meat is at least 165 degrees.)*

Glaze bbq jerk sauce on the pork and rest on cooler parts of the grill. Close grill and cook for 10 minutes.

Take pork off grill. Use a sharp knife and cut pork joint into small cubes and serve.

FLAVA TIP
TRY WITH

~~~~~~

Rice & peas
Macaroni cheese
Great for family events and BBQ's

JAMAICAN BEEF PATTIE

It's great if you're on-the-go, and it tastes even better when it's freshly baked. You can choose to fill your Pattie with grounded beef mince, chicken or saltfish, and combine it with the spices below to satisfy you to the max!

TIME: 2 HOURS 15 MINUTES | SERVES: 6

INGREDIENTS

450g of flour*

2 tsp sugar

1 tbsp vegetable oil

1 ½ tsp salt

5 tbsp of turmeric powder

2 tbsp of shortening or lard

2 tbsp of butter**

1lb of ground mince beef

1 tsp of salt

1 tsp of black pepper

1 medium onion *(diced)*

1 scotch bonnet pepper *(chopped)*

½ tsp of garlic powder

1 tsp of paprika

1 tsp of pimento seeds or all spice

2 beef stock cubes

150ml of water

1 tsp breadcrumbs or flour

2 tbsp soy sauce or worcestershire sauce or browning sauce

DIRECTIONS

For the pastry:

Sieve the flour into a bowl and then add salt, sugar and tumeric. Mix together and then add butter and shortening. Mix until it forms a crumbly texture.

Gradually add ice cold water and mix until it forms a dough. Roll the dough into a ball and wrap in cling film. Leave it in the fridge for 1 hour

For the beef mince:

Pour vegetable oil in a frying pan on high heat, then fry onions and scotch bonnet pepper for 3 mins. Then add the ground beef mince and cook until brown. Add salt, garlic powder, black pepper, beef stock cubes (mixed with water), paprika, all spice, flour or breadcrumbs and soy sauce. Stir well and simmer for 20 mins. Taste and adjust the seasoning if necessary.

After 1 hour, take your dough out of the fridge. Place some flour on the surface and roll your dough flat, and then fold over 2-3 times and repeat.

Once rolled out, place a medium-sized bowl on the dough and carefully cut around it. (Cut as many as you can.)

Then, using a tablespoon, add a spoonful of beef mince to the centre of the pastry. Brush some milk around the edge of the dough to help you seal the pattie.

Carefully fold the pattie so that the ends meet and use your finger to seal it together. Press a fork into the edge of the dough. And then gently poke holes on the top of the pattie.

Carefully place patties on a baking tray and put into a pre-heated oven at 180 degrees for 25 minutes until golden brown. *(It should be soft but firm on the outside.)*

Let the patties rest for 30 minutes, then serve.

Healthier Flava

*Gluten-free flour
**Dairy free butter
Remove sugar and salt
Use a vegetable filling

COCO BREAD

A sweet bread that is adored by caribbeans for its combination as a sandwich with the Jamaican pattie. We used to enjoy grabbing one of these from the local caribbean shop on-the-go as it filled us up for most of the day – and it tasted so good!

~~~~~~~~~~

TIME: 2 HOURS | SERVES: 6

INGREDIENTS

2 tbsp of melted butter**
1 x 400g tin of warm coconut milk
500g of plain flour*
A likkle bit of salt
1 tbsp of sugar
2 tbsp of shortening
125ml of warm water
3 tsp of quick-rise yeast
1 tbsp olive oil

DIRECTIONS

Pre-heat oven to 180 degrees.

In a bowl, mix together the flour, sugar, salt and yeast.

Mix the water and coconut milk together on the stove until it's warm and then add melted butter. Pour this into the flour and add shortening. Mix until the dough is soft and smooth.

Sprinkle some flour onto your worktop surface. Then knead the dough into a ball. Brush olive oil and butter over the dough and then cover with Cling-film. Leave it to sit for 1 hour so it can rise.

Once the dough has risen, uncover and sprinkle more flour onto your worktop surface. Roll out the dough and fold over 3 times.

Cut it into pieces to make individual coco bread pieces. Roll each one, making sure it has a slight thickness. Brush butter on the dough.

Cut out a bowl shape on the dough and fold over into a semi circle, then let it sit for 10 minutes for the dough to rise. Repeat to make more.

Place on a baking tray and put in a pre-heated oven at 180 degrees for 15 minutes or until dough is golden brown.

Once ready, let it rest for an hour, cut open and place a pattie inside and enjoy!

FLAVA TIP
TRY WITH
~~~~

Jamaican pattie

Healthier Flava
Gluten-free flour
***Dairy free butter*
Remove sugar and salt

DOUBLES

The ultimate traditional trini street-food. This delicious curry channa *(curry chick peas)* sandwiched between bara – a sweet flat bread – offers a filling on-the-go tummy pleaser. Bwoii, it taste good!

~~~~~~~~~

TIME: 2 HOURS | SERVES: 6

INGREDIENTS

2 tbsp of corn starch or corn flour
450g of flour*
2 x 400g tins of chickpeas
2 tablespoons of curry powder
1 medium onion *(diced)*
4 cloves of garlic *(chopped)*
1 tsp of salt
2 spring onions *(chopped)*
2 tbsp of turmeric powder
Vegetable oil
250ml of water
1 tbsp of yeast

Optional sauce toppings:
Channa (chickpeas) Tamarind sauce, cucumber chutney.

DIRECTIONS

Soak chick peas in water overnight.

Add the flour to a bowl with the turmeric powder, salt and yeast and then mix together.

Gradually add the warm water to flour and knead until it forms a dough ball. *(The dough should be soft and sticky so add more flour or water until it's right.)*

Cover with Cling-film and let the dough sit for 1 hour.

For the Channa:

Drain the soaked chickpeas and season with garlic, onion, black pepper, spring onions and mix together.

On a high heat, add vegetable oil to a pot and then stir in the curry power. Cook for 2 minutes.

Turn to medium heat. Then add chickpeas to the pot and cook for 5 minutes. Pour in 2 cups of water and bring to the boil.

To thicken the sauce, add corn starch or cornflour and mix together and simmer for 15 minutes until thick.

For the Doubles:

Add vegetable oil to your dough. Break off some dough and roll into a small ball. Gently make a circular-shaped.

Heat vegetable oil in a pot and deep-fry doubles for 30 seconds. Once done, place on a paper towel and cover.

Mash the chickpeas and stir.

Serve doubles with Channa (chickpeas) Tamarind sauce, cucumber chutney.

Healthier Flava
*Gluten-free flour

DIRTY JERK BURGER

Quick and tasty juicy jerk burger filled with melted cheese, onions and drenched in jerk bbq sauce. The ultimate guilty pleasure.

~~~~~~~~~~~~~~~~~

TIME: 40 MINS | SERVES: 1-2

INGREDIENTS

250g of ground mince beef

Sliced cheese

1 tbsp of jerk paste

Jerk BBQ sauce

1 tsp of jerk seasoning

Burger buns

Lettuce

¼ of small red onion *(cut in rings)*

¼ of small onion *(cut in rings)*

1 tbsp vegetable oil

DIRECTIONS

Put ground minced beef in a mixing bowl and massage jerk paste and jerk seasoning into the meat. Then mould into the shape of a burger.

Alternatively, buy ready-made minced burgers and massage with jerk paste and jerk seasoning.

Grill on each side until cooked to your preference.

Cut onions and red onions in rings and dash in a frying pan. Sauté in vegetable oil until onions are well done.

Paint burger buns with butter and grill for 20 seconds on each side.

Place a fresh lettuce leaf on the base of the burger bun, then the minced burger, slice of cheese, onions and a layer of jerk bbq sauce. If ya bad, top it up with another burger!

Serve burger with your favourite toppings.

FLAVA TIP
TRY WITH
~~~~~~

Plantain fries

FRIED JERK SEASONED CHICKEN WINGS

Crunchy fried chicken wings marinated with jerk seasoning. Yum!
This is Caribbean style street-food at it's best – you'll love it! Give it a
try and tell us what you think on social media.

~~~~~~~~~~~~~~~~~~

TIME: 30 MINUTES | SERVES: 5-7

INGREDIENTS

Water

Lemon

1 tsp baking powder

2 tsp of all purpose seasoning

1 pound of chicken wings

2 beaten eggs

250g flour*

2 tbsp of jerk paste

1 tsp of black pepper

A likkle bit of salt

Vegetable oil *(enough to deep-fry)*

DIRECTIONS

Wash the chicken wings with lemon and water, and cut into drums and flats *(at the joint)*, also cutting off the tip.

In a mixing bowl, season with salt, black pepper, jerk paste and all purpose seasoning.

Beat 2 eggs and pour over the chicken.

Add the baking powder, all purpose seasoning and flour and then mix together.

Dip the chicken wings into the flour mix making sure it's fully coated.

Pour the vegetable oil into a pot making sure there's enough to deep-fry the chicken wings. Put it on high heat. Once heated, lower to medium. Fry the chicken wings for until golden brown.

Once done, place chicken wings on paper towel to soak up the excess oil.

FLAVA TIP
Great for sharing with friends and family

Healthier Flava

Gluten-free flour

SWEET CHILLI BAKED WINGS

These sweet, sticky wings will spicy up ya life! This is one of our most flavasome on-the-go snacks. You'll love it!

TIME: 45 MINUTES | SERVES: 4

INGREDIENTS

1 pound of chicken wings
1 tbsp of all purpose seasoning
1 tsp of baking powder
1 tbsp of butter
1 tsp of corn starch or cornflour
1 tsp of black pepper
A likkle bit of salt
2 tbsp of soy sauce
2 tbsp of sweet chilli paste
250ml of sweet chilli sauce
A pinch of thyme
Vegetable oil
Lemon
Water

DIRECTIONS

Wash the chicken wings with lemon and water, and cut into drums and flats *(at the joint)*, also cutting off the tip.

Season wings with salt, thyme, pepper and all-purpose seasoning. Mix it together and then cover with cling film. Tip: Marinate for a couple of hours for extra flava!

Preheat oven to 180 degrees. Place wings on a baking tray and bake for 25 minutes, turning them half-way through.

For the sauce:

Melt butter in a frying pan on a high heat.

Add sweet chilli sauce, cornstarch or corn flour, baking powder, sweet chilli paste and soy sauce and fry for 5 minutes. Reduce to a medium heat.

Take the wings out of the oven after 25 minutes and add them to the sauce mix. Stir in the sauce and simmer for 5 minutes.

Then place the chicken wings onto a baking tray and cook in the oven for 10 minutes at 180 degrees.

Garnish with thyme and serve.

FLAVA TIP

Great for sharing with friends and family

CARIBBEAN RUM PUNCH

Bwoiii this drink is the ultimate summer cocktail! A refreshing alcoholic punch with a delicious tropical taste. A blend of fruit juices and mixture of rums combined together to make the perfect sweet tasting drink to get the party started! *Drink responsibly, of course.*

~~~~~~~~~~

TIME: 10 MINS | SERVES: 4

INGREDIENTS

Ice
125ml of grenadine or strawberry syrup
4 limes
A pinch of nutmeg
500ml of orange juice
500ml of pineapple juice
100ml shots of coconut rum
100ml shots of dark rum
100ml shots of white rum
2 litre jug and a stirring spoon
1 orange *(sliced)*
1 lime *(sliced)*

DIRECTIONS

Add the ice first, then white rum, dark rum and coconut rum.

Pour in the orange juice, pineapple juice, and squeeze the limes in. Stir with a spoon.

Gradually add in the grenadine or strawberry syrup, *(Take a snap on your phone of the gradient colour the cocktail makes. It looks nice, bredrin!)*

Dash in slices of orange and lime. Pour, drink and taste the refreshing Caribbean flavas! Ya mon!

FLAVA TIP

Don't fancy alcohol? Remove the rum and you'll have a delicious fruit punch!

drinkaware.co.uk
for the facts

GINGER BEER

Traditional Jamaican ginger beer is a naturally sweetened and carbonated beverage. You can make it with or without alcohol. This drink is made with natural ginger and sugar, which gives it a strong a sweet taste.
(No harm in adding a likkle rum!) Drink responsibly, of course.

TIME: 20 MINS | SERVES: 2

INGREDIENTS

140g of fresh ginger

1 clove

2 whole limes

100g of sugar

500ml of sparkling
or spring water

A big jug and a stirring spoon

Optional:
Likkle bit of rum

DIRECTIONS

Peel the ginger and cut into small pieces. Put it in the blender with 1 clove.

Add the sugar, lime juice, white rum and water into the blender. Blend for 3-4 minutes.

Optional: Put sugar on a plate, press cup rim on the sugar and turn slightly.

Serve with ice and lime.

PINA COLADA

Most famous as the ultimate holiday cocktail! Well, now you can make it from the comfort of your home. Rum is a major ingredient in this one (no surprise there). So give it a try and pretend you're on a tropical island. Ya mon!

~~~~~~~~~~~~~~~~~~

TIME: 10 MINS | SERVES: 2-4

INGREDIENTS

150ml coconut milk
6 ice cubes
100ml of dark rum
100ml of white rum
100ml of coconut rum
250ml of pineapple juice
150g of pineapple chunks
2 tsp honey or syrup or sugar

Decorations
1 pineapple quarter slice
Straw
Umbrella toothpick
Cherry

DIRECTIONS

Place the following into a blender:

Dash in ice, dark rum, white rum, coconut rum, pineapple juice, pineapple chunks, honey and coconut milk.

Blend until frothy and then:

Decorate glass for one with 1 cherry thrown in and a slice of pineapple on the edge of the glass. Use umbrella toothpick and straw – if you want to.

FAMILY BLESSING

GOD bless this family
with joy and peace
let thy love abide here.

Bless each one in this family
with faith to build their life anew.

Bless all with good health and success
to fill this house with happiness.

Jamaica

NANNY'S YARD

Growing up Caribbean, everyone knows that when you go to Grandma's house, you're in for a feast. Whatever the occasion, Grandma always provides the best Caribbean food and drink to fill ya belly!

▶ Check out video recipes on originalflava.com

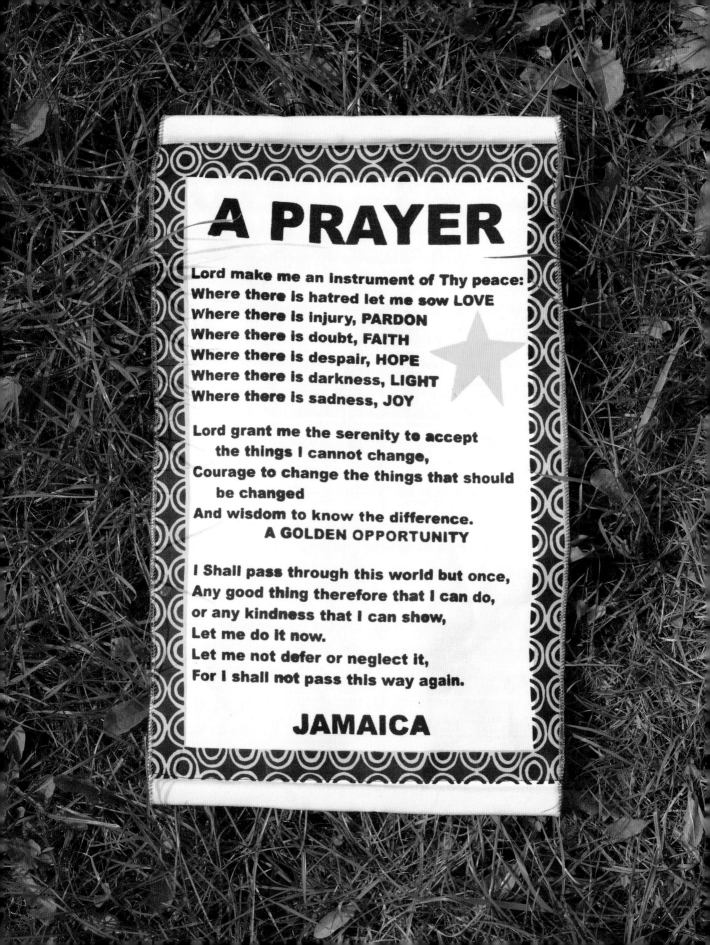

A PRAYER

Lord make me an instrument of Thy peace:
Where there is hatred let me sow LOVE
Where there is injury, PARDON
Where there is doubt, FAITH
Where there is despair, HOPE
Where there is darkness, LIGHT
Where there is sadness, JOY

Lord grant me the serenity to accept
    the things I cannot change,
Courage to change the things that should
    be changed
And wisdom to know the difference.
        A GOLDEN OPPORTUNITY

I Shall pass through this world but once,
Any good thing therefore that I can do,
or any kindness that I can show,
Let me do it now.
Let me not defer or neglect it,
For I shall not pass this way again.

JAMAICA

BROWN STEW CHICKEN

Tasty chicken stew dish, caribbean style! Soaked in a rich and thick gravy, this dish has plenty of spicy flavas to indulge on.

TIME: 1 HOUR | SERVES: 5-6

INGREDIENTS

3lbs of chicken legs and thighs
1 tsp of browning or soya sauce
2 tbsp of vegetable oil
1 tsp paprika
1 tsp salt
1 tsp black pepper
1 tsp salt
1 tsp fresh thyme
2 garlic cloves
½ medium red bell pepper *(sliced)*
½ medium green bell pepper *(sliced)*
3 spring onions *(chopped)*
1 medium onion *(chopped)*
500ml of water
1 tsp of ginger
1 scotch bonnet *(chopped)*
1 tbsp of ketchup or 1 large fresh tomato
½ tsp of cornstarch or flour
Lemon

Optional:
1 tsp salt flavour enhancer
1 tsp butter
hot pepper sauce

DIRECTIONS

Wash chicken with lemon and water. Remove skin and slit chicken with knife to enable the seasoning to marinate inside the chicken.

Place chicken in a mixing bowl, add salt, spring onion, paprika, half of the bell peppers, black pepper, fresh thyme and garlic. Marinate in fridge overnight.

Scrap off the spring onion and bell peppers from chicken and set aside. Pour vegetable oil to pan on medium heat. Once hot, add chicken to pan and cook untill brown.

Remove the chicken and some of the oil out of the pan. Add the remaining bell peppers and spring onion. Including the ingredients that were scrapped off after marinating overnight. Also, add the chopped onion, ginger, scotch bonnet, fresh thyme and cook for 3 minutes

Once that is cooked, dash in a likkle salt, tomato ketchup, browning, water and cornstarch to make a thick gravy.

Place the chicken back in the pan, cover and simmer for 40 minutes at medium heat. Add more water if necessary.

FLAVA TIP
TRY WITH

Rice & peas

Healthier Flava
*Rapeseed oil

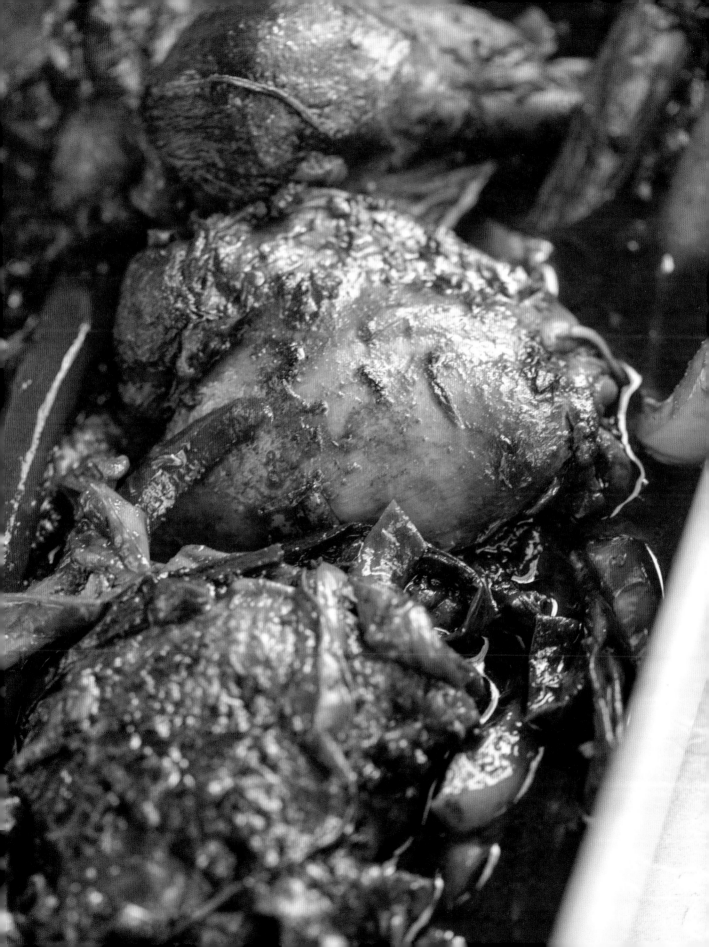

CURRY GOAT

One of the Caribbean's most famous dishes. It's rich blend of spices will leave you craving more! We've made this an E.A.T. recipe so you can enjoy this tasty treat. It's perfect for dinners with loved ones.

~~~~~~~~~~~~~~~~~~~~

TIME: 3 HOURS | SERVES: 6

INGREDIENTS

3 pounds of goat or mutton
1 tsp of all purpose seasoning
4-5 tbsp of curry powder
3 cloves of garlic (finely chopped)
1 large onion (chopped)
1 tsp of ginger powder
1 tsp of black pepper
1 tsp of pimento seeds
8 baby potatoes (chopped in half)
1 tsp of salt
2 spring onions (chopped)
3 sprigs of fresh thyme
1 whole scotch bonnet pepper
4 tbsp of vegetable oil
500ml water
400ml of coconut milk

DIRECTIONS

Wash goat meat with water and lemon.

Put goat meat in a bowl and add 2 tablespoons of curry powder, salt, black pepper, ginger, pimento, all purpose seasoning and marinate meat in fridge for up to 8 hours (optional).

Heat oil in a large pot and add 2 teaspoons of curry powder, onions, garlic and cook for 2-3 minutes.

On medium high heat, put goat meat into pot and cook until brown.

Then add water and coconut milk to the pot. Cover and cook for up to 2 hrs stirring every 20 mins, until meat is tender (low-medium heat).

Add spring onion and fresh thyme, baby potatoes and scotch bonnet pepper. Then boil for 15 minutes.

Take out scotch bonnet pepper (leave in longer for a more spicy taste)

Cover the pot, and cook for 30 minutes more until meat is falling off bone. Add more water if necessary.

FLAVA TIP

Use a pressure cooker to shorten cooking time to 1 hour

TRY WITH

Rice & peas
Coconut rice
White rice

CURRY CHICKEN

Chicken marinated with a combination of spicy curry flavas.
This is one of the most loved curries in the caribbean. Try it out
and you'll see why!

TIME:1 HOUR | SERVES: 4-6

INGREDIENTS

2 medium carrots (chopped)

3 pound of chicken breast (cubed)

1 tsp of all spice or chicken seasoning

200ml of coconut milk

4 tbsp of curry powder

1 tsp of tumeric

2 tsp of ginger powder

1 medium onion *(chopped)*

2 tbsp of vegetable oil

1 tsp of paprika

1 tsp of garlic powder or cloves

1 tsp of black pepper

1 tsp of pimento seeds or powder

8 baby potatoes *(chopped in half)*

A likkle bit of salt

4 branches of fresh thyme

1 small scotch bonnet *(chopped)*

DIRECTIONS

Wash the chicken with water and lemon and cut into medium sized cubes. Season with 2 tablespoons of curry powder, 1 tsp of ginger, tumeric, garlic, salt, black pepper and paprika. Marinate overnight.

Pour the oil into a frying pan and place on a medium-high heat. Once heated, fry the onions, garlic and scotch bonnet pepper for 3 minutes.

Add 2 tablespoons of curry powder and 1 tsp of ginger to the pot. Stir and cook for 3 minutes. Add a likkle water.

Add the chicken to the pan and cook until brown.

Pour in the coconut milk and stir. Then add the pimento, fresh thyme, carrots, peeled potatoes, then cover and boil for 20-30 minutes.

FLAVA TIP

TRY WITH

Rice & peas
Coconut rice
White rice

PUMPKIN & SWEET POTATO CURRY

A delicious dish perfect for vegans or vegetarians.

~~~~~~~~~~~~~~~~

TIME: 30 MINUTE | SERVES: 4-6

INGREDIENTS

1 tsp of chilli powder

2 tbsp of curry powder

3 cloves garlic

1 tsp of ginger (finely chopped)

2 tbsp of olive oil

1 medium onion (diced)

1 tsp of paprika

200g of parsley or callaloo

1 tsp of black pepper

1 scotch bonnet pepper

3 sweet potatoes (peeled & diced)

500g pumpkin or butternut squash (diced)

A likkle bit of sea salt

2 spring onions

1 tsp of turmeric

400ml of coconut milk

DIRECTIONS

On a high heat, add olive oil to your pot and fry curry powder for 2 minutes. Then add your onions, garlic, scotch bonnet pepper, spring onions and fry for another 2 minutes.

Add the pumpkin and sweet potatoes and season with black pepper, paprika, chilli powder, turmeric powder, ginger, and mix together.

Pour in the coconut milk and stir. Cook until the pumpkin is tender.

Add parsley or callaloo and simmer for 5 minutes.

ESCOVITCH FISH

This is a traditional Jamaican Easter dish. Every year, we looked forward to Grandma making us a big batch. Although it's typically made around that time of the year, there's always an excuse to make this delicious dish. Go on, you won't regret it.

TIME: 50 MINUTES | SERVES: 2

INGREDIENTS

2 whole red snapper or any fresh fish of your choice
Water
Lemon or lime juice
2 medium carrots *(finely cut)*
1 tsp of fish seasoning
3 cloves of garlic *(chopped)*
1 lemon or lime
½ a medium onion *(sliced)*
Vegetable oil* *(to shallow fry)*
1 tsp of black pepper
½ medium red bell pepper *(sliced)*
½ medium green bell pepper *(sliced*
½ medium orange bell pepper *(sliced)*
1 scotch bonnet pepper *(chopped)*
1 tsp of pimento seeds
A likkle bit of salt
4 branches of fresh thyme
125ml of white vinegar

DIRECTIONS

For the fish:

Firstly wash and clean fish with water, lemon/lime and vinegar inside and out and then pat until it's dry.

Score the fish on each side and season with salt, black pepper and fish seasoning. (Make sure you season inside the fish too.)

Pour oil into a non-stick frying pan on a high heat.

When cooking oil is hot, carefully place the fish in the pan and cook for 10 minutes on each side until it's crispy and golden brown.

Remove fish and set aside on a paper towel to remove excess oil.

Pour out some of the oil. Then use what's left in the pan to make the dressing.

For the escovitch dressing:

On medium–high heat, add onion rings, carrots, peppers, fresh thyme, pimento seeds, garlic and scotch bonnet pepper and cook for 3 mins.

Add vinegar and mix together.

Dash in some salt and pepper and cover the pan. Let it simmer for 10 mins.

Serve fish on plate and garnish with escovitch dressing.

FLAVA TIP
TRY WITH

Hard dough bread
Coconut rice
Rice
Bammy
Festival
Fried dumpling

FLAVA TIP

Ask fish monger to clean and scale fish

Healthier Flava

*Rapeseed oil
Place fish in oven rather than deep frying.

FRIED FISH

You can now eat your Escovitch fish with no interuptions (bones!).
It's our cod or haddock fillet seasoned with spicy and flavaful batter.
Add some chips (fries), and you've got fish and chips with a
Caribbean Twist! Yes iyah.

~~~~~~~~~~~~~~~~~~~~~~~

TIME: 40 MINUTES | SERVES: 4

INGREDIENTS

2 tbsp of all purpose seasoning
2 medium carrots *(sliced)*
1 pound of cod fillet or haddock fillet
2 eggs *(beaten)*
2 tbsp of fish seasoning
250g of flour
70ml cup of milk
1 onion *(sliced)*
2 spring onions *(sliced)*
2 tsp of paprika
2 tbsp of black pepper
¼ medium red bell pepper *(sliced)*
¼ medium green bell pepper *(sliced)*
¼ medium yellow bell pepper *(sliced)*
1 tsp of pimento seeds (crushed)
Vegetable oil *(enough to shallow fry)**
125ml of white vinegar

DIRECTIONS

For the fish:

Season your fillet with all purpose seasoning, paprika, black pepper and fish seasoning and set aside.

Then add all purpose seasoning, paprika, black pepper and fish seasoning to your flour and mix together.

Beat eggs and add milk to mixture. Whisk and pour onto the fish fillets and let it sit for 5 minutes.

Use a frying pan on high heat and add vegetable oil.

Cover the fish in flour and shake off the excess.

Fry in pan on each side until golden brown.

Pour out some of the oil. Then use what's left in the pan to make the dressing.

For the escovitch dressing:

Add onion, carrots, bell peppers, spring onions, scotch bonnet, pimento seeds, and scotch bonnet pepper to the frying pan.

Add black pepper and vinegar and then let it simmer for 10 minutes.

Garnish on fish.

FLAVA TIP
TRY WITH
~~~~~~~~~~

Hard dough bread
Rice & peas
Bammy
Festival
Fried dumpling

Healthier Flava

*Rapeseed oil

BROWN STEW FISH

Whole snapper fish steamed down in a delicious Jamaican stew.
It's an alternative to our Brown stew chicken for those of you
who don't eat meat. And it's just as tasty.

TIME: 50 MINUTES | SERVES: 2

INGREDIENTS

1 tsp of browning sauce*
2 medium carrots (sliced)
2 snapper fish (cut in half)
1 tsp of fish seasoning
1 tsp of all purpose seasoning
a likkle bit of salt
1 medium onion (sliced)
2 spring onions (sliced)
1 tsp of black pepper
1 scotch bonnet pepper
4 sprigs of fresh thyme
Vegetable oil**(to shallow fry)
125ml cup of vinegar
¼ medium red bell pepper (sliced)
¼ medium green bell pepper (sliced)
¼ medium yellow bell pepper (sliced)
Lemon or lime

DIRECTIONS

Firstly wash and clean fish with water, lemon/lime
and vinegar inside and out and then pat until it's dry.

Season snapper with black pepper, likkle bit of salt, all
purpose seasoning and fish seasoning.

Add oil to a frying pan and place on a high heat.
Once hot, turn to medium heat. Fry the fish for 10
minutes on each side until golden brown and then
place on a paper towel.

Using the same pan and oil, add the onions, carrots,
spring onions, thyme, scotch bonnet pepper and sauté.

Place the snapper back into the pan, add browning
sauce and vinegar and simmer for 10 minutes.

TRY WITH

Hard dough bread
White Rice
Bammy
Festival
Fried dumpling

FLAVA TIP

Ask fish monger to clean and scale fish

Healthier Flava

*Soy sauce
**Rapeseed oil

JERK SEASONED SALMON w/ MANGO SALSA

Delicious modern day dish with a caribbean twist. The spicy jerked seasoning and sweet mango salsa provides a beautiful combination of flavas.

〜〜〜〜〜〜〜〜〜〜

TIME: 35 MINS | SERVES: 2-4

INGREDIENTS

Water

Lemon

140g x 4 salmon fillets

2 tsp of fish seasoning

1 tsp of honey

2 tsp of jerk seasoning

1 tbsp of jerk paste
(or make your own jerk marinade, see recipe on page 71)

250g of mango *(chopped)*

1 tbsp of olive oil

1 tbsp of vegetable oil

1 medium onion *(diced)*

150g of pineapple *(chopped)*

1 tsp of black pepper

½ medium red bell pepper *(sliced)*

½ medium green bell pepper *(sliced)*

1 scotch bonnet pepper

A likkle bit of salt

DIRECTIONS

Wash the salmon with water and lemon and then slit 2-3 lines into the skin.

In a bowl, add jerk paste, jerk seasoning, fish seasoning and water.

Massage marinade into the salmon and rest on the side.

Pour vegetable oil in a frying pan on high heat.

Once hot, turn down to medium. Fry the salmon on both sides for 5 minutes. Then place onto a baking tray and cook for a further 10 minutes at 180 degrees.

Mango salsa:

Mix the following in a bowl; mango, pineapple, scotch bonnet pepper, bell peppers, honey, onions, lime juice, salt, black pepper and oil. Put in fridge for 30 minutes.

Garnish salsa on top of salmon.

FLAVA TIP
TRY WITH

Coconut rice
Stir fry veg

Healthier Flava

Rapeseed oil

CURRY SHRIMP

One of Craig's favourites: it's a flavalicious dish that can be used as a main or a side. The shrimp's marinated in a thick, coconut curry stew.

~~~~~

TIME: 30 MINUTES | SERVES: 4

INGREDIENTS

2 tbsp of curry powder

125ml of coconut milk

2 cloves of garlic (chopped)

1 of a tsp of ginger

1 medium onion (chopped)

¼ medium red bell pepper (sliced)

¼ medium green bell pepper (sliced)

1 scotch bonnet pepper (chopped)

1 tbsp of ketchup

1 pounds of king prawns or shrimp (de-shelled)

1 tsp of black pepper

1 tsp of salt

1 tsp of cornstarch

1 tsp of vegetable oil

125ml of water

1 tsp of thyme

DIRECTIONS

Season shrimp with black pepper, salt and curry powder and then set aside.

Add vegetable oil to a frying pan and put on a high heat. Then add onions and curry powder and saute for 3 minutes – reduce to a medium heat.

Add ginger, garlic, scotch bonnet, thyme, sweet mixed peppers and stir well. Cook for a further 2 minutes and then add ketchup, water and coconut milk. Simmer for 3 minutes.

Mix water and cornstarch together and add to pan. Simmer for 1 minute.

Then add shrimp or king prawns and cook for 5-10 minutes.

BBQ FRIED CHICKEN

Packed with spicy flavours and a sweet BBQ glaze on top of a crispy coating, this BBQ fried chicken is sure to get your mouth watering. We're postive it'll be finger-licking good!

TIME: 1 HOUR | SERVES: 5

INGREDIENTS

Lemon

Water

1 tsp salt

3lb of chicken legs

1 tsp of black pepper

1 tsp paprika

1 tsp ginger

1 tsp barbecue seasoning

2 tbsp of all purpose seasoning

2 beaten eggs or milk

1 tsp of chilli powder

Vegetable oil *(to mid-shallow fry)*

1 medium onions *(chopped)*

2 tbsp of ketchup

4 tbsp of bbq sauce

½ a lime squeezed

200ml pineapple juice

500g of plain flour

1 tsp of baking powder

½ scotch bonnet (remove seeds)

FLAVA TIP
TRY WITH

Coconut rice

DIRECTIONS

Wash chicken with lemon and water.

In a mixing bowl, add salt, black pepper, paprika, ginger, barbecue seasoning, all purpose seasoning and marinate in fridge for up to 6 hours.

Take bowl out of the fridge, add 2 beaten eggs and massage together. Let chicken sit for 30 mins.

In a separate flat bowl, throw in flour, baking powder and all purpose seasoning. Roll chicken into flour until totally covered.

Frying chicken

Pour vegetable oil in a frying pan, enough for a shallow fry on high heat. Once heated, gently place chicken into frying pan and turn to medium heat. Fry chicken until golden brown on each side.

Once finished, place chicken on paper towels laid on top of a plate to dry excess oil.

Making the sauce

Place a frying pan on medium heat and add bbq sauce, chilli powder, squeeze of lime juice and pineapple juice, and stir until seasoning cooks down.

Roll fried chicken into bbq sauce and completely cover chicken with it. Then place chicken on a baking tray and put in pre-heated oven for 5-10 mins. This makes the sauce sticky and gives it a nice gloss.

COCONUT FRIED CHICKEN

The best fried chicken you'll ever have, with a Caribbean twist!
The coconut and curry flavours are often the perfect couple, and it doesn't disappoint in this one. You've GOT to try it!

TIME: 45 MINUTES | SERVES: 6-8

INGREDIENTS

Vegetable oil (enough for a deep fry)*
Water
Lemon
4 tbsp of all purpose seasoning
1 pound of chicken drumsticks
250ml coconut milk
4 tbsp of curry powder
450g of flour**
2 tsp of ginger
2 tsp of paprika
2 tsp of black pepper
A likkle bit of salt
2 tsp of thyme

Optional:
2 beaten eggs to liquid mix

DIRECTIONS

Wash the chicken with water and lemon and then season with some of the all purpose, curry powder, salt, paprika, black pepper, ginger, thyme and coconut milk.

Mix together and let it marinate for a minimum of 2 hours.

Add flour in a bowl then mix in black pepper, all purpose, curry powder, thyme, and paprika.

Then coat the chicken with the flour and set aside.

Pour the oil into a deep pot and place on a high heat.
(There should be enough oil to deep-fry the chicken.)

Fry a few pieces of chicken at a time until it's golden brown for around 10-15 minutes***.

Place a kitchen towel on a plate to drain the excess oil.

Once they're all fried, put the chicken onto a baking tray and bake in the oven for 15 minutes at 180 degrees

FLAVA TIP
TRY WITH

Rice & peas
Coconut rice

---Healthier Flava---

*Rapeseed oil
** Gluten-free flour
***Bake in oven for 45 minutes in oven instead of frying

OVEN-BASED JERK SEASONED CHICKEN

Traditionally, jerk chicken is cooked in a jerk pan and smoked with pimento wood. However, for those located in colder environments – like we are in England – we've created an oven-based recipe that tastes just as good as the original!

~~~~~~~~~~~~~~~~

TIME: 50 MINUTES | SERVES: 4-6

INGREDIENTS

4 chicken leg quarters

2 tbsp of jerk seasoning

4 tbsp of jerk marinade/paste

(or make your own jerk marinade, see recipe on page 71)

DIRECTIONS

Wash chicken with lemon and water and pat dry.

Slit chicken, place in a large mixing bowl and add jerk seasoning and jerk paste. Massage into chicken and then marinate in the fridge overnight.

After marinating, place chicken on baking tray and cook in pre-heated oven for 45 minutes at 180 degrees. Chicken should be dark brown and slightly crispy.

FLAVA TIP
TRY WITH
~~~~~~~

Rice & peas
Macaroni and cheese
Coconut rice

MEET NANNY

I was born in the Red lands in Clarendon, Jamaica, in 1935. It was in the countryside where everyone was friendly and would give you the last penny in their wallet if you needed it. I came to England in 1955 when I was only 20 years old. Ya mon, young girl! Back then, people from Jamaica could come over easily.

I got married in 1957 in Brixton town hall. It was a nice wedding, mon. We had big up food like curry goat, rice and peas and all dem ting deh. Our caterer was really nice and gave us a good deal on the food, but me cyan't 'member her name. But Sidney – mi husban' – would ah remember.

Times back then was very tough! There were places with signs that said 'No Blacks or Irish allowed', so we couldn't go to certain places. But I won't name and shame. We had to stay in a house with five other people we didn't know! We shared the same toilet, bathroom and kitchen with them. You had

to wake up really early so that you could be the first one to use the cooker otherwise you had to wait for a long time. Our room cost £1 a week to rent in Brixton on Geneva road. That, and Somerleyton road, were the two baddest roads in Brixton – but now, it so nice! Times ah change, suh!

We used to go to the market to buy all the food we needed. And we still do. But back then, if you were down on money, this one and that one would lend you £50. Ya mon, everybody affi eat!

We moved from Geneva road and stopped at a couple of friends' house for a while, in and around Coldharbour lane in Brixton where Craig and Shaun's mother was born. We then moved to Tulse Hill and then, not long after, we bought our first house in Balham in 1970. We stayed there for over 20 years.

We made so many memories of all the children dem. All six of my likkle children grew in that house, turned into big people and then left to set up their own homes. But they would come back and let my grandchildren stay. My favourite thing to cook for them was porridge in the morning – they loved it. Not the oats kind, though, ah cornmeal porridge dem love!

We celebrated lots of Christmases and birthdays in that house. Nuff people and good food, mon. Though, it was tough raising the children dem on my own. But when them sick, I help dem, and when them bad, I still love them. They, and God, were my strength! His grace and mercy brought me through.

Nanny's Favourite Dish
Mackerel Rundown

NANNY'S COLD & FLU REMEDY

In desperate need to get rid of your cold? This recipe can help! We're sharing grandma's TWO best ever 'cure' for our colds. For the record, Grandma isn't a doctor and, as far as we know, didn't study medicine either. But we've never seen her with a cold...

HOT REMEDY

INGREDIENTS

30g of fresh ginger *(crushed)*

2 slices of lemon, plus the juice of 1/2 lemon

Sweeten with honey *(until you're happy with the taste)*

150ml Water

DIRECTIONS

Get a small pan and throw some water in it and bring to a boil. Crush ginger, cut slices of lemon, squeeze lemon juice and dash it in the boiling water.

Boil for 5 minutes and squirt some honey in it to sweeten. Pour into a mug and see that cold go away!

REMEDY SHOT!

INGREDIENTS

Honey

White rum

1 medium lemon *(½ squeezed and ½ sliced)*

DIRECTIONS

You can drink it in one go but white rum burns your chest. We suggest you spoon-feed yourself to avoid choking. Also, taking it a bit at a time gives it time to work – at least that's what grandma says.

You should be extremely wrapped up when taking this – I'm mean: jumper, dressing gown and quilt or blanket – so you can sweat buckets. If you take this before bed (as it will most likely knock you out), this will help you feel completely different – without the hangover.

We're not sure what the combination of rum, honey and lemon is about *(Nanny's secret, maybe?)*, but we know whenever we've taken it, that niggling cold disappears.

Give it a try but don't take this before you're about to drive or use machinery – Grandma would not approve.

JUICY ROAST CHICKEN

The ultimate sunday roast king-pin. This recipe oozes with juicy flava!
For those who struggle with their roast coming out dry, follow this
recipe and it won't happen to you!

~~~~~~~~~~~~~~~~~~~

TIME: 2 HOURS | SERVES: 6-8

INGREDIENTS

1 tbsp all purpose seasoning
1 tbsp of butter
2 large carrots *(chopped)*
1 tbsp chicken seasoning
1 extra large whole chicken
1 tbsp of olive oil
1 large onion *(chopped)*
2 spring onions *(chopped)*
1 tbsp of paprika
10 baby potatoes *(chopped)*
4 sprigs of fresh thyme
1 red bell pepper
1 green bell pepper
2 chicken stock cubes

DIRECTIONS

Wash your chicken with lemon, water and pat dry.

Poke holes into the chicken using a sharp knife.

Combine all purpose, chicken seasoning, and paprika into a
bowl. Mix together and then rub it inside the chicken.

Score the onion and insert into the chicken cavity with the
spring onion and add fresh thyme.

Melt the butter and rub all over chicken. Drizzle some olive
oil over it too.

Put the potatoes, bell peppers and carrots into a large baking
tray and drizzle a likkle olive oil on top. Then place your
whole chicken on top.

Make sure you tuck the wings under the chicken and tie
the legs together with cooking string.

Cook in 180 degree oven for 1.5 hours in the middle tray.
(To make gravy, add chicken stocks to the juices from chicken
and add ½ cup of hot water and stir.)

HONEY ROASTED LAMB

Bwoii, this one is di ting! A tender leg of lamb with a honey glaze for a sunday dinner = heaven in our household. We're sharing this secret recipe with you and your family to enjoy!

~~~~~~~~~~~~

TIME: 1 HOUR 45 MINS | SERVES: 8-10

INGREDIENTS

1 tbsp of all purpose seasoning
2 lamb stock cubes
Lime
2 Spring onions *(chopped)*
125ml water *(for lamb stock cubes)*
1 tbsp of butter
2 carrots *(chopped)*
1 tablespoon of flour
6 cloves of garlic
125g of honey
2.4kg leg of lamb
1 cup of olive oil
2 onions *(chopped)*
1 tbsp of paprika
1 tbsp of black pepper
1 whole yellow bell pepper
1 whole red bell pepper
10 baby potatoes
A likkle bit of salt
6 sprigs of fresh thyme

DIRECTIONS

Pre-heat the oven to 160 degrees.

Wash the lamb with water and lime and then poke 1-2cm holes all over the lamb.

Rub the olive oil all over and then add salt, pepper, all purpose and paprika.

Place the garlic cloves, spring onions and fresh thyme into some of the holes.

Pour the honey over the lamb and set aside.

Add the onions, carrots, sweet peppers and baby potatoes to a baking tray and drizzle oil and honey over them. Then sprinkle with black pepper.

Place the lamb on top of the vegetables and then cook in the oven for 1 hour and 30 minutes (if you want it medium) or cooked to your liking.

Take out the lamb and let it cool for a little while.

Place the baking tray on the stove and add the broth, flour or corn starch and mix it together to make gravy.

Slice your lamb and serve with the vegetables and gravy.

FLAVA TIP
TRY WITH
~~~~

Rice & peas

PEPPER STEAK

A stir-fried Jamaican dish. Sliced beef steak cooked with colourful sweet bell peppers and carrots, seasoned with spicy herbs and a thick gravy to glaze the meat. Be careful. It spicy, mon!

~~~~~~~~~~

TIME: 1 HOUR | SERVES: 4

INGREDIENTS

2 pounds of steak *(cut into strips)*
Water
1 tsp paprika
3 spring onion *(sliced)*
2 tbsp of all purpose seasoning
1 tsp of all spice or pimento seeds
125ml of beef broth
1 tbsp of cornstarch or flour
4 cloves of garlic
1 tbsp of olive oil
1 medium onion *(sliced)*
1 tbsp of black pepper
1 scotch bonnet pepper *(chopped)*
A likkle bit of salt
1 tbsp of soy sauce or browning
1 tbsp of thyme.
2 medium carrots *(sliced)*
¼ medium green bell pepper *(sliced)*
¼ medium red bell pepper *(sliced)*
¼ medium orange bell pepper *(sliced)*
¼ medium yellow bell pepper *(sliced)*

DIRECTIONS

Wash the beef with lemon and water and then cut into strips.

Season with salt, black pepper, thyme, paprika, all purpose and marinate overnight.

Place a pan on a medium-high heat and add the oil. Then fry the onions, garlics and scotch bonnet pepper for 3 minutes.

Spoon the fried ingredients into a bowl and then cook the beef in the same pan. Brown the beef for 10 minutes.

Add all spice or pimento seeds and the beef broth.

Add soy sauce and the pre-fried ingredients into the pot and cook for 5 minutes.

Add the bell peppers, spring onions carrots, cornstarch and mix together.

Leave to simmer for 30 minutes until the meat is tender.

SALTFISH FRITTERS

The sight and smell always excites us – they're that good. Nothing beats coming downstairs for breakfast or a family gathering to the sight of these bad boys on the dining table. Crispy, flavasome and easy to make! You'll love them. It's a tasty, on-the-go snack!

~~~~~~~~~~

TIME: 40 MINUTES | SERVES: 5

INGREDIENTS

½ a tsp of baking powder
500g plain flour
Vegetable oil *(enough for shallow fry)*
1 medium onion *(chopped)*
1 tsp of paprika
1 tsp of black pepper
1 of scotch bonnet *(chopped)*
2 small tomatoes *(chopped)*
350g of boneless saltfish cod
3 spring onions *(sliced)*
¼ green bell pepper *(diced)*
¼ red bell pepper *(diced)*
250ml of water
1 tsp of garlic
1 tsp of thyme
1 tsp of all purpose seasoning

Optional
Hot pepper sauce

DIRECTIONS

You'll need to start by removing the salt from the saltfish.

You can either boil it in water for 10 minutes, drain it and repeat twice, or you can soak it in cold water overnight and then drain 2 or 3 times during the night and refill with water.

Once that's done, shred the saltfish into small pieces and then put it into the mixing bowl.

Add baking powder, onion, scotch bonnet, paprika, black pepper, garlic, thyme, all purpose seasoning, spring onions, sweet peppers and chopped tomato into the bowl and then add water.

Dash in the 4 cups of plain flour and mix everything together. *(The mixture should be a sloppy consistency)*

Place your frying pan on a high heat and add your oil.

Scoop in a large serving spoon of the mixture per fritter into the oil and fry for around 5 minutes on each side, until golden brown.

CARROT JUICE

We loved Grandma's carrot juice growing up, it tasted like a milkshake; sweet and flavasome. This drink is traditionally made on the weekend as it's seen as a special treat – and trust me, it's very special.

~~~~~~~~~~~~~~~~~~~

TIME: 20 MINS | SERVES: 4

INGREDIENTS

2 pounds of peeled carrots
1 tsp of cinnamon
400g of sweet condensed milk*
1 tsp of nutmeg
1 tsp of vanilla essence
1 litre of water

Optional
100ml of white rum

DIRECTIONS

Wash and peel carrots and then put them in the blender or food processor. Add water and blend until smooth.

Sieve the carrot juice into a bowl. Squeeze the carrots in the sieve to get more juice and then stir the liquid.

Add sweet condensed milk, cinnamon, nutmeg, vanilla essence, white rum and stir thoroughly.

Serve with ice.

Healthier Flava

*Coconut milk, almond milk or soya milk

GUINNESS PUNCH

Ya-gah yo! This is one of Shaun's favourite things! It goes down a treat with the family on Christmas Day! This creamy, sweet milk is complemented by the strong, bitter Guinness kick. It's great to sip on after a flavasome dinner! Yum!

~~~~~~~~~~~~~~~~~~~~

TIME: 10 MINS | SERVES: 6

INGREDIENTS

4 x 440ml cans of Guinness
1 tsp of cinnamon
400g of sweet condensed milk or Vanilla milk drink*
1 tsp of nutmeg
1 tsp of vanilla essence
Large jug and a stirring spoon

DIRECTIONS

Pour Guinness into a blender or large jug.

Add sweet condensed milk, nutmeg, cinnamon, vanilla essence and stir.

Serve with ice.

PEANUT PUNCH

The drink that packs a powerful, protein punch. It's the perfect pick-me-up wherever you are. You'll be nuts not to try it!

INGREDIENTS

1 tsp of cinnamon
250g sweet condensed milk*
250g peanuts
1 tsp of sugar
1 tsp of vanilla or honey
250ml of water

DIRECTIONS

Blend all these ingredients together until smooth and serve with ice.

~~~~~~~~~~~~~~~~~~~~

TIME: 10 MINS | SERVES: 2

Healthier Flava
Coconut milk, almond milk or soya milk

CARIBBEAN SORREL DRINK

We normally drink this traditional, refreshing drink during the festive season. It's Infused with sorrel plant petals, rum, ginger, and sugar to sweeten. The process along with ingredients provides an authentic and full taste.

~~~~~~~~~~~~~~~~~~~~~~

TIME: 10 MINS | SERVES: 4

INGREDIENTS

1 tsp of cinnamon

3oz of grated ginger

4 cloves

1 tsp of lemon juice

5 whole pimento seeds

400g of dry petal seeds

400g of sugar

1.8 litre cups of water

A likkle bit of white rum *(to your preference)*

DIRECTIONS

Wash the sorrel and place in a large pot.

Pour 10 cups of water over the sorrel and add all the ginger, pimento seeds, cloves and cinnamon and bring to the boil. Stir well while it's boiling.

Turn off the fire after 5 minutes and then leave it to rest.

Once it's cool, add a few orange peels (optional) and place the sorrel in the fridge overnight.

When you're sure it's cold, sievethe sorrel into a bowl. You'll need to squeeze the sorrel remains in the sieve to get the maximum juice out.

Add the sugar, lime and rum, and stir until the sugar has dissolved.

Serve with ice once you've let it rest in the fridge for a few days. You'll thank us when you taste it ;)

"Dis sorrel SWEET, MON!"
— Nanny

SATURDAY SOUPS & STEWS

Every Saturday was soup or stew day in most Caribbean households! A selection of hearty soups to take you through the weekend.

 Check out video recipes on originalflava.com

BEEF SATURDAY SOUP

You can change the main ingredient of Saturday soup to suit your mood. Choose either beef, lamb, mutton or chicken. This recipe includes tender beef cooked down in a wholesome soup with vegetables.

~~~~~~

TIME: 1 HOUR 30 MINUTES | SERVES: 5

INGREDIENTS

1 tsp of black pepper
2 spring onions *(chopped)*
1 tsp of all spice/pimento
3 carrots *(chopped)*
250g of flour
2 pounds of stewing beef *(diced)*
3 leeks *(chopped)*
2 x 50g packet of pumpkin soup mix
1 large onion *(chopped)*
250g of pumpkin *(diced)**
A likkle bit of salt
1 whole scotch bonnet
3 medium sweet potatoes *(chopped)*
4 sprigs of fresh thyme
250g of yam
2 small corn on the cob
1 litre of water

Optional:
Butter
2 beef stock cubes

DIRECTIONS

Boil water and throw in stewing beef, pumpkin, black pepper and salt. Cover and boil for 1 hour on medium – low heat.

Add chopped carrots, leeks, corn on the cob chopped in half, pimento seeds, spring onions, and fresh thyme. Stir well.

Add sweet potatoes, yam and boil for further 15 minutes.

For the dumplings (see page 36 for dumpling recipe)

Tear off a small piece of dough and roll it into a small ball dumpling or spinner *(thin worm shape)* and add it to the soup. Then, add scotch bonnet pepper and boil for 15 minutes.

Then add the pumpkin soup mix, and simmer for 5 – 10 minutes

OXTAIL STEW

Juicy fall-off-the-bone comfort food. This tender meat bathed in a thick stew, is one of the most loved Jamaican dishes. You'll soon see why once you dive into it.

~~~~~~~~~~~~~

TIME: 3 HOURS 30 MINS | SERVES: 6

INGREDIENTS

3 pounds of oxtail**
2 tbsp of all purpose seasoning
Lemon
1 tsp of salt
1 beef stock cube
400g of butter beans
2 tbsp of cornflour or corn starch*
1 tsp of garlic powder
1 onion (chopped)
1 tsp of black pepper
1 scotch bonnet pepper (chopped)
5 pimento seeds
3 spring onions (chopped)
2 tbsp of soy sauce or browning
3 sprigs of thyme
2 tbsp of vegetable oil***
1 litre of water
2 medium carrots (chopped)

DIRECTIONS

Wash Oxtail with water and lemon.

Season with salt, pepper, thyme, pimento seed, garlic, all purpose seasoning and browning. Then marinate overnight.

On a high heat, add cooking oil to a frying pan and then brown the oxtail for 15 minutes.

Remove the meat and leave to rest in a side dish. Then add more oil to the pan and fry the onions, spring onions and scotch bonnet pepper for 5 minutes.

Add the oxtail back to the pan with the remaining marinade and then add fresh thyme.

Pour in water and beef stock cube and stir well. Cook for 2.5 hours on a medium-high heat and stir every 30 minutes.

Add cornflour or corn starch to thicken the gravy. Stir well.

Add carrots and let it simmer for 30 minutes. (Add more water if you need)

At this stage, the meat should be falling of bone and very tender. If it's not, cook it for longer.

Finally, add butter beans and cook for a further 5 minutes.

Healthier Flava

* Add more vegetables to thicken stew instead of cornstarch.
** Cut fat off oxtail
*** Rapeseed oil

FLAVA TIP

- Use a pressure cooker to shorten cooking time to 1 hour 30 minutes
- Add boiled dumpling and cook for 20 minutes towards the end.

GROWING UP CARIBBEAN

We fondly remember our upbringing. As children of Caribbean descent, there were a few things that we experienced growing up. We're sure you can relate to a few.

1. YOU HAD TO CLEAN *Every* SATURDAY MORNING

Lie-ins didn't exist. And you could forget about watching cartoons too. The house had to be cleaned from top to bottom and there was no escaping it. Sometimes, it would even run into the afternoon when you had plans. You just had to suck it up and clean without looking miserable.

2. *Waking* UP TO THE SMELL OF FOOD!

The weekend hadn't started unless the smell of something amazing woke you up with a smile. If you were really lucky it was a full-on breakfast of ackee & saltfish with fried dumpling. This dish would keep you satisfied for most of the day.

3. SINGING WHILST COOKING = FEAST FOR DINNER

The chef of the house would either hum or sing when they cooked. That was a sign that it was about to go down in the kitchen. Once the singing began, the smell of food filled the house. On the odd occasion though, the sweet-smelling food was for someone else.

4. SNEAKING IN THE KITCHEN TO EAT FROM *Dutch Pot*

Yes. We all did it even though we were strictly told not to touch the pot until it was dinner time. We couldn't help ourselves. It was the same routine every week: you ran to get a fork or spoon, tiptoed back to the pot and helped yourself to whatever was inside.

5. YOU COULDN'T USE ANYTHING IN THIS CABINET

You'll never forget the 'good' crockery that only surfaced once a year; two if you're lucky. In fact, they're probably still there now. And don't get us started on the plates with the gold rim that couldn't go in the microwave!

6. THE LIVING ROOM WAS ONLY FOR SPECIAL GUESTS

The living room was almost always locked and you never knew where the key was. But when the doorbell rang, your parents ushered guests in the living room. And you, sadly, weren't invited to join.

7. THE ICE CREAM CONTAINER THAT NEVER HAD ICE CREAM IN IT

You 100% wanted the Neapolitan ice cream but instead you got leftovers from some time or another. And then you lost hope in there ever being real ice cream in the freezer. The disappointment was real! Word of warning: don't trust the ice cream tub.

BEEF STEW

This tender beef stew is a delicious comfort food. Packed with hearty root vegetables, you'll find yourself going back to this recipe to cook for loved ones, again and again.

~~~~~~~~~~

TIME: 1 HOURS 20 MINS | SERVES: 5

INGREDIENTS

2 tsp of all purpose seasoning
2 pounds of stewing beef* (cut in pieces)
2 beef stock cubes
2 tsp of browning or soy sauce**
2 medium carrots (chopped)
300g of flour
4 cloves of garlic
1 medium onion (chopped)
1 tsp of paprika
1 tsp of black pepper
1 scotch bonnet pepper
A likkle bit of salt
4 spring onions (chopped)
4 branches of fresh thyme
500ml of water
1 tbsp of vegetable oil***

DIRECTIONS

Wash the beef with water and lemon and then cut into pieces.

Season with soy sauce, salt, black pepper, all purpose seasoning and paprika. Let it marinate in the fridge for at least 2 hours.

Pour the oil into a deep pot and place on a high heat. Fry the onions, garlic and spring onions for 3 minutes.

Reduce to a medium heat, add the beef and brown for 10 minutes.

Mix the stock cubes with two cups of boiling water and then add to the pot. Stir well.

Add fresh thyme and then cook the beef for 45 minutes (with the pot lid on) until the meat is tender.

(The sauce will reduce and thicken slightly. You can add ½ a cup more of water if you want to.)

For the dumplings (see page 36 for dumpling recipe)

Tear off a small piece of dough and roll it into a small ball dumpling, or spinner *(thin worm shape)* and then add it to the soup and boil for 15 minutes.

Add carrots, and scotch bonnet pepper and let it simmer for another 15 minutes.

Healthier Flava

* Cut fat off beef
** Use soy sauce
*** Rapeseed oil

ITAL SOUP

Ital is VITAL! This dish is loved by rastafarians because of its natural plant based ingredients. A very healthy dish and it taste wicked mon! So much flava, so much goodness! *Suitable for Vegans*

~~~~~~~

TIME: 1 HOUR | SERVES: 5

INGREDIENTS

2 chopped green bananas
60g basil leaves
280g of callaloo or spinach or kale
1 small cho cho *(chopped)*
500ml of coconut milk
2 medium carrots *(chopped)*
3 cloves of garlic
A likkle bit of grated ginger
1 tsp of thyme
1 medim onion *(chopped)*
150g of okra
150g of chick peas
1 tsp of ground black pepper
1 tsp of pimento or all spice
1 large white potato
1 large sweet potato
250g of pumpkin *(chopped)*
1 whole scotch bonnet
A likkle bit of sea salt
3 spring onions *(chopped)*
3 sprigs of fresh thyme
1 litres water

DIRECTIONS

Wash the chick peas, put them into a large pot and pour water into the pot. Bring to a boil on a medium heat. Leave for 30 minutes – or when you feel the peas are soft.

Lowering the heat, add the garlic, ginger, onions, black pepper, pimento, sea salt, spring onions, and thyme. Stir together.

Raise to a medium heat again and add the carrots, cho cho, okra, potato, sweet potatoes and pumpkin.

Stir in 2 cups of coconut milk, callaloo and scotch bonnet and let it simmer for 40 minutes.

STEW PEAS

A truly traditional and hearty Jamaican stew. Don't let the name fool you, though. There's more beef and pig's tail than kidney beans, which gives it an amazing flava. We used to look forward to this meal whenever Grandma made it for us! Enjoy.

TIME: 1 HOUR 10 MINUTES | SERVES: 5-7

INGREDIENTS

1 tsp of all purpose seasoning
1 x 400g tin of red kidney beans
½ a pound of stewing beef
½ a cup of carrots *(chopped)*
1 x 400g tin of coconut milk
1 tbsp of corn starch or cornflour
250g plain flour
4 cloves of garlic *(chopped)*
1 medium onion *(chopped)*
2 spring onions *(chopped)*
1 tsp of paprika
1 tsp of black pepper
1 whole scotch bonnet pepper
4 sprigs of thyme
500ml of water

Optional
2 beef stock cubes
½ a pound of pig's tails

DIRECTIONS

Soak the red kidney beans in a pot of water overnight. *(If you use pig's tails, soak it.)*

Season the stewing beef with black pepper, all purpose seasoning and paprika and then marinate overnight.

Using the same pot you used to soak the red kidney beans in, add the stewing beef *(and pig's tails)* with 2 cups of water. Cover with pot lid and cook for 30 minutes until meat is tender.

Add the tin of coconut milk and stir well.

Then add the spring onions, fresh thyme, garlic, onions, scotch bonnet pepper, carrots and mix together. Cook for 15 minutes.

Make your dumplings *(see dumpling recipe on page 36)* and roll them into thin sausages shapes. Put them into the pot and let it simmer for another 15 minutes.

To thicken the stew, add the corn starch or cornflour and mix it together. Or you can add 2 beef stock cubes.

CHICKEN PUMPKIN SOUP

The traditional Jamaican 'Saturday soup'. Growing up in a Jamaican household, you'd have this dish at least one saturday a month with the family. A Perfect winter-warmer pick me up! We're sure it cured every cold or temperature we had growing up!

~~~~~~~

TIME: 50 MINUTES | SERVES: 8

INGREDIENTS

1 cup of green banana
2 medium carrots (chopped)
1 cup of cho cho (chayote)
1 packet of chicken noodle mix
1 pound of skinless chicken on the bone (chopped)
500g of flour
1 medium onions (chopped)
2 spring onions (chopped)
1 tsp of black pepper
1 tsp of garlic
200g potatoes or sweet potatoes
250g pumpkin (diced)
1 x 50g pack of pumpkin soup mix
1 x 50g packet of cock soup mix
A likkle bit of salt
1 scotch bonnet
4 sprigs of fresh thyme
150g yam
1.8 litres of water

Optional:
Chicken stock cube
Corn on the cob
Plantain

DIRECTIONS

Add water to a large pot and bring to the boil.

Cut the chicken into pieces. Dash in the chicken, pumpkin, salt, garlic and black pepper. Then boil for 20 minutes.

Turn down to medium heat, and add chopped carrots, spring onions, cho cho, black pepper and thyme.
Stir everything together.

Wash and add potatoes, yam, green banana and boil for further 15 minutes.

For the dumplings (see page 36 for dough recipe)

Tear off a small piece of dough and roll it into a small ball dumpling or spinner (thin worm shape). Then, add it to the soup. Add scotch bonnet pepper and boil for 15 minutes.

Add the pumpkin and cock soup mix packets and boil di ting for a further 5-10 minutes

Serve in soup bowls, kick back and as we say 'nyam!' *(eat)*

RED PEA SOUP

One of the most recognisable soups to come out of Jamaica. Full of dumplings, juicy beef, yam, sweet potato and hot spices, it's sure to warm your stomach and fill you up! You can use pig's tails or turkey neck as a base flava for this soup – it's really down to you.
As Caribbean's say, 'just go with what you have!'

~~~~~~

TIME: 1 HOUR 30 MINUTES | SERVES: 8

INGREDIENTS

1 tsp of all spice or pimento
1 pound of stewing beef
2 medium carrot (chopped)
1 pound of pig's tail*
1 packet of cock soup mix
1 x 400g can of coconut milk
250g flour**
3 gloves of garlic (chopped)
1 medium onion (chopped)
3 spring onions (chopped)
2 x 400g cans of red kidney beans
1 tsp of black pepper
A likkle bit of salt
1 whole scotch bonnet
1 sweet potato (chopped)
1.8 litre of water
100g of yam (chopped)
4 sprigs of fresh thyme

Optional

*You can use a turkey or chicken leg/neck – it's just for additional flavour

DIRECTIONS

Soak your red kidney peas in a pot overnight in 8-10 cups of water. Also soak pig's tails in separate pot in cold water overnight.

When you're ready, put the peas on a low fire so it begins to boil.

Wash and boil pig's tail in a separate pot for 10 minutes. Rinse and repeat twice until salt is removed. Once done, add it to the main pot.

Add your chosen meat to the peas and bring it to the boil on a medium heat.

Add salt and pepper, then add your beef and cook until all the meat is tender. (This should take 1 hour.)

After this, add the onions, spring onions, pimento, scotch bonnet and fresh thyme and then stir well. (Don't forget, take out the scotch bonnet in 20 minutes before it bursts)

Add the carrots, cock soup packet, coconut milk, sweet potato, yam and dumplings (see boiled dumpling recipe on page 36). Tear off piece of dough, and rub between hands to make a small sausage shape and throw in soup.

Stir well and then let it simmer for 15 minutes.

SWEET TREATS

Growing up, when we were well behaved, we'd always be rewarded with one of these delicious treats! If you have a sweet tooth, you'll love these Caribbean inspired recipes.

▶ Check out video recipes on originalflava.com

SPICED BUN & CHEESE

Easter bun is must in a Caribbean household during Easter – we'd eat it with thick slices of cheddar cheese. Every year we'd see huge lines at the caribbean bakery for this sweet snack. So to avoid the queues, we learnt how to make it. And you should do the same!

~~~~~

TIME: 1 HOUR 30 MINUTES | SERVES: 8

INGREDIENTS

2 tsp of baking powder
1 tsp of browning sauce
500g of butter
1 tsp of cinnamon
100g of glace cherries
1 beaten egg
400g of plain flour
250g of mixed fruits
1 tsp of mixed spice
1 tsp of guava jam*
1 teaspoon of nutmeg
250ml of red label wine
A likkle bit of salt
284ml of stout
250g of brown sugar
1 tbsp of vanilla essence

DIRECTIONS

Flour mix:
Mix together the flour, cinnamon, nutmeg, salt, baking powder, mixed spice and set aside.

Liquid mix:
On a high heat, melt the butter in a pot and then add the red wine, stout, sugar and vanilla essence. Keep mixing until it's all dissolved and then turn the fire off so it can cool down. *(Pour it into a separate bowl and leave for 10 minutes.)*

Add the beaten egg to the liquid mix and stir.

Pour half of the flour mix into the liquid mix, then pour in half of the mixed fruits and cherries and fold. Pour in the remainder of the flour mix, mixed fruit and cherries and fold again.

Add the guava jam and browning sauce and then mix together until it's sloppy.

Grease your deep baking tin with butter or vegetable oil, and carefully pour in the mixture.

Place the tray in the middle of the oven and let it bake for 1 hour in a pre-heated oven at 180 degrees.

Once finished, let it cool for 1 hour, cut and serve with sliced cheese.

FLAVA TIP

Test whether the cake is done by poking a toothpick into the bun, and if the stick comes clean and dry, it's ready to nyam!

MANGO & PINEAPPLE CRUMBLE

Every sweet-tooth lover's dream dessert. This Caribbean crumble combination with either custard or ice cream gives a feeling that can't be matched. It's Flavalicious!

~~~~~~~~

TIME: 1 HOUR 15 MINUTES | SERVES: 8

INGREDIENTS

10 digestive biscuits *(crushed)*
120g cup of butter *(room temperature)*
1 tsp of cinnamon
400g of plain flour
250g of mango chunks
125ml mango juice
1 tsp of nutmeg
125g of oats
125ml of orange juice
250g of pineapple chunks
125ml of pineapple juice
2 tbsp of corn starch
120g of sugar *(2 tbsp for the fruits)*
1 tsp of vanilla essence

DIRECTIONS

For the crumble:

Add flour and butter to the bowl and mix together with your hands until it's crumbly.

Then add the biscuits, oats and sugar and then mix it all together to create the perfect crumble. Leave it to rest on the side.

For the puree:

On a high heat in a non-stick pan, pour in the mango, orange and pineapple juice. Then add 2 tablespoons of sugar and corn starch, the cinnamon, nutmeg and vanilla and let it boil. *(It should be quite thick.)*

Place your fruits into a deep baking tray and then pour the puree over the fruits.

Then, with your hands, crumble the topping over the fruits. Make sure it's evenly spread.

Cook for 45 mins at 200 degrees until the crumble is golden brown.

BANANA FRITTERS

A sweet finger-food with a soft and fluffy texture. This sweet treat is tasty whether you eat it on it's own or with something else. We love ours with a bowl of vanilla ice cream. My mouth is watering thinking about it! Try it now - you won't regret it!

TIME: 20 MINUTES | SERVES: 4-6

INGREDIENTS

4 over-ripe bananas
120g of sugar
250g of plain flour
2 tsp of vanilla essence
½ tsp of cinnamon
½ tsp of nutmeg
½ tsp salt
1 tsp of baking powder
Vegetable oil (enough to shallow fry)*

DIRECTIONS

Crush the bananas in a bowl, add sugar and mix together. Once mixed, fling vanilla, cinnamon, nutmeg, salt and mix together. Add flour and mix well.

Pour cooking oil in frying pan on high heat. Using a large spoon, carefully pour the mix onto frying pan, making a medium sized circular shape. Repeat allowing room in the frying pan.

Turn heat down to medium and fry for 3 minutes on each side until golden brown. Once finished, dry fritters on paper towel and serve

FLAVA TIP

Don't throw away over-ripe bananas, they can still be used to make this dish.

SWEET POTATO PUDDING

Sometimes known as 'hell a top, hell a bottom and hallelujah in the middle'. A sweet traditional dessert with a soft texture. It's great with ice cream or cream.

~~~~~

TIME: 2 HOURS MINUTES 15 | SERVES: 8

INGREDIENTS

750g sweet potatoes *(chopped)*
300g of brown sugar
250g of plain flour
125g of fine cornmeal
1 tsp of mixed spice
1 tsp of nutmeg
1 tsp of salt
1 t of baking powder
1 tbsp butter
400g of coconut milk
100g of raisins
250ml water

Optional:
100g of yam
1 tsp of browning

DIRECTIONS

Pre-heat oven 180 degrees.

Pour water inside a pot, place sweet potatoes inside and boil until they soften.

Then grab a large bowl and add plain flour, fine cornmeal, mixed spice, nutmeg, salt, baking powder, and mix together.

Add coconut milk and butter then add your raisins, browning *(optional)*. Mash the sweet potato, add to the mix and stir well.

Butter up a deep round baking tin/tray and add some greaseproof paper inside.

Pour your mixture into the baking tin/tray and cook for 1.5 hours at 180 degrees. Then let it cool down for 30 minutes

FLAVA TIP

Test whether the cake is done by poking a toothpick into the bun, and if the stick comes clean and dry, it's ready to nyam!

CARROT CAKE

This is our mouth-watering carrot cake – we do it a likkle different in the Caribbean. Indulge and enjoy this fluffy sweet treat with friends and family.

~~~

TIME: 1 HOUR 15 MINUTES | SERVES: 8

INGREDIENTS

1 tsp of baking powder
1 tsp of baking soda
400g of carrots (grated)
1 tsp of cinnamon
4 medium eggs (unbeaten)
400g plain flour
1 tsp of nutmeg
250g raisins
A likkle bit of salt
350g of brown or white sugar
1 tbsp of vanilla essence
250ml vegetable oil

DIRECTIONS

Pre-heat the oven to 180 degrees.

Whisk together the eggs, sugar, vanilla essence and vegetable oil and then set aside.

In a separate bowl, mix the nutmeg, cinnamon, flour, baking powder, baking soda and salt. Then fold the wet mix into this. *(You can add carrot or orange juice if you think the mixture is too dry.)*

Add the carrots and raisins and then mix together.

Grease a deep baking tray with butter and pour in the mixture. *(It should half-fill the baking tin so that the cake can rise without spilling over.)*

Place in the centre of the oven and bake for 45 minutes until it's golden brown.

Once cooked, leave it to cool and serve with cream cheese frosting on top.

FLAVA TIP

Test whether the cake is done by poking a toothpick into the bun, and if the stick comes clean and dry, it's ready to nyam!

PLANTAIN PANCAKES

Thick and tasty American Pancakes topped with plantain & syrup.
This combination compliments perfectly, and is a really simple recipe
that will get your tastebuds bouncing!

TIME: 30 MINUTES | SERVES: 5

INGREDIENTS

1 tbsp of baking powder
30g of melted butter
2 large eggs (beaten)
225g of plain flour
300ml milk
1 tsp of vegetable oil or butter*
A likkle bit of salt
1 tsp of brown or white sugar
1 tsp of vanilla essence
2-3 plantains

DIRECTIONS

Pour the milk into the blender and then add melted
butter, beaten eggs, plain flour, milk, salt, sugar, and
vanilla essence. Blend until the mixture is thick and
smooth. Then let it rest for 15 minutes.

Add the oil to a non-stick frying pan and use a tissue to
spread the oil around the pan. Put the pan on a medium
heat.

Once the pan is hot, pour the pancake mix into the
middle of the pan. Move the pan so that the mix makes a
circular shape.

Cook all pancakes for 1 minute on both sides.

Add some more oil to the pan (so that you can shallow fry
the plantain) and wait until it gets hot.

Turning the heat down to a medium heat, add the plantain
and fry on each for 2-3 minutes until it's golden brown

Decorate your pancake with plantain and syrup.

Healthier Flava
* Coconut oil
Don't use sugar

COCONUT DROPS

A traditional Jamaican sweet treat, filled with caramelised sugar and grated coconut.

~~~~~~~

TIME: 1 HOUR 30 MINUTES | SERVES: 5

INGREDIENTS

500g of coconut pieces
1 tbsp of grated ginger
250g of sugar
1 tsp of vanilla
1 tsp of cinnamon
1 litre of water

DIRECTIONS

Boil 4 cups of water in a pot and add the coconut pieces.

Let them cook for 30 minutes until they're soft.

Add sugar and ginger to the pot and mix together. Boil it until the mixture is caramelized.

Add cinnamon and vanilla to give some flava, then simmer for 30 minutes.

Butter up a large baking tray, then add 1 tablespoon of coconut drop mixture and carefully drop onto the tray.

Let it cool for 15 minutes.

GIZZADAS

Gizzada or Gizzarda, is an open tart pastry filled with grated sweetened coconut pieces. It's a fun filled tasty snack to eat.

~~~~~~

TIME: 30 MINUTES | SERVES: 5

INGREDIENTS

500g of flour
50g of butter
50g of shortening
125ml of water
1 large coconut *(inside grated)*
250g of brown sugar
1 tsp of nutmeg
2 tbsp of water

DIRECTIONS

Sieve the flour into a large bowl and add the butter and shortening.

Work the butter and shortening into the flour until the mixture is crumbly. Then, gradually add cold water and knead dough into a ball.

Wrap in Cling-film and put it in the fridge for 30 minutes. Break the coconut and grate the coconut meat. Then add it to a frying pan on a high heat.

Add sugar, nutmeg, butter, and water. Mix together and let it simmer for 15 minutes.

Roll out the pastry on the worktop surface and cut out medium-sized circles.

Use your fingers and shape the pastry into a star. Spoon the coconut mixture into the middle.

Place on a baking tray and put it in the oven for 15 minutes at 180 degrees.

RUM BLACK CAKE

This rum infused cake is an ever-present in the Jamaican household during the festive season. The soaking of the dried fruit in white rum and red label wine is the most sacred part. The longer you soak, the richer the taste! A great dessert to share with family and friends!
Do not serve to children.

~~~~

TIME: 1 HOUR 30 MINUTES | SERVES: 10-12

INGREDIENTS

500g of brown sugar

500g of butter or margarine

10 eggs

450g of plain flour

2 teaspoon of baking powder

1 tsp of nutmeg

1 tsp of cinnamon

1 tsp of salt

1 tsp of all spice

1kg of mixed dried fruits soaked in white rum and red wine

1 tsp vanilla essence

1 tsp of lemon juice

60ml of browning sauce

Optional:
Cracker crumbs

REMEMBER

Soak mixed dried fruits in white rum and red label wine for at least 2 weeks prior to starting this recipe.

FLAVA TIP

Test whether the cake is done by poking a toothpick into the bun, and if the stick comes clean and dry, it's ready to nyam!

DIRECTIONS

Butter mix:

Mix together 1 cup of brown sugar and 500g of butter/margarine until you get a creamy fluffy consistency.
(It's easier with a hand-mixer.)

Add eggs one by one. Mix everything together each time you add an egg. Do this until the mixture's runny.

Dry ingredients:

In a separate bowl, add plain flour, baking powder, nutmeg, all spice, cinnamon and salt. Mix together. Sieve half of this mix into the butter mix and fold.

Pour half of the mixed fruits soaked in rum and mix well until smooth. Then pour in lemon juice, vanilla essence, 1 shot of white rum and browning.

Add remainder of mixed fruits and blend together with hand-mixer.

Grease a deep baking tin with butter. Then pour mixture into baking tin until it's half the height of the tin. This allows the cake to rise while cooking. Shake until evenly separated.

Pre-heat your oven to 180 degrees and put the cake in for 1.5 hours.

Once finished, dash a likkle more rum on top of the cake for a glaze and garnish with Christmas decorations.

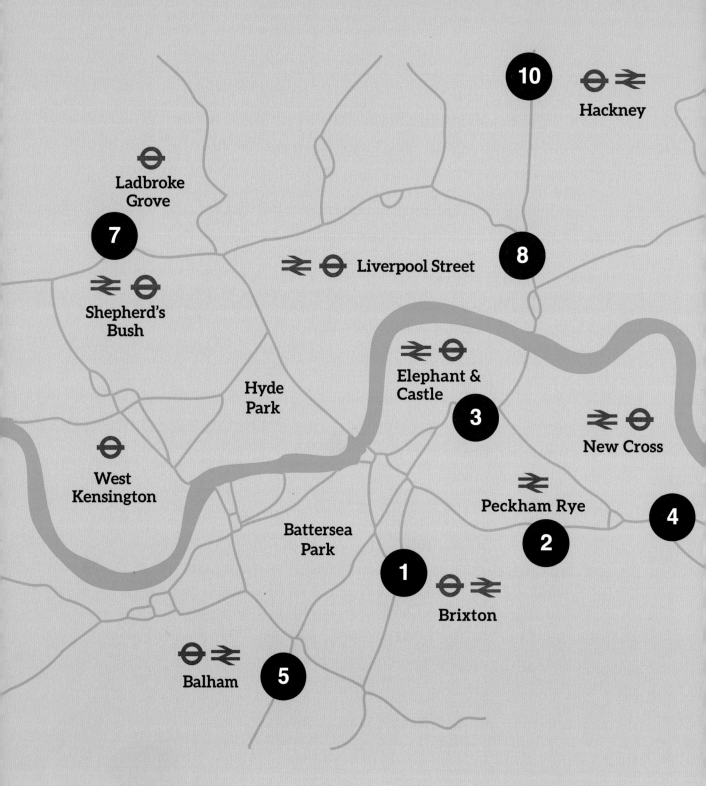

Ladbroke Grove

7

Shepherd's Bush

10

Hackney

Liverpool Street

8

Elephant & Castle

3

New Cross

Hyde Park

West Kensington

Peckham Rye

4

2

Battersea Park

1

Brixton

Balham

5

10 MARKETS AROUND LONDON

10 markets around London where you can buy your Caribbean ingredients.

1. Brixton Market

Brixton station road SW9
Mon, Tues, Thurs, Fri 8am-6pm
Wed 8am-3pm, Sat 8am-5.30pm

2. Choumert Market

Choumert Road Peckham SE15
Monday-Saturday 9am-3pm

3. East Street Market

East Street Market SE17
Mon, Tues, Wed, Sat 8am-5pm
Thurs, Friday 9am-5pm

4. Lewisham Market

Lewisham High Street SE14
Monday-Saturday 9am-4pm

5. Hildreth Street Market

Hildreth Street SW12
Monday-Saturday 7am-6pm

6. Tooting Market

Upper Tooting Road SW17
Mon, Tues, Thurs-Sat 9am-5pm
Wed 9am-1pm

7. Portobello Market

Portobello Road W11
Monday-Sunday 9am-3pm

8. Petticoat Lane Market

Middlesex Street E1
Mon-Fri 10am-2pm
Sun 9am-2pm

9. Shepard's Bush Market

Goldhawk Road W12
Monday-Saturday 9am-5pm

10. Ridley Road Market

Ridley Road R8
Monday-Saturday 7am-5pm

INDEX

ACKNOWLEDGEMENTS

We'd like to say a big thank you to those who pledged towards our kickstarter campaign, to help make this book a reality.

And special thanks to the following for their contributions:

Mike Clare, Paul Morrison, Tina Lee, Thomas Colwell, Gerard Kevin Mbeumo
Gladesmore Secondary School, Tottenham, London, UK, (*Teachers*) Juliet Coley & Antuneil Thompson (*Students*) Abdullah Cokgezici, Jibreal Hersi, Mohamed Hussien, Warsame Ibrahim, Rimel Lawrence, Revon McGann, Elliot Osbourne-Monaghan, Dylano Richards-Wright, Denzel Sergeant-Gammon, Nathan Scott and Ra'Shane Thornhill-Yearwood.

Premises credits:
Cornfields bakery, Thornton Heath, UK; p20-1, 78-9
Jerk centre Thornton Heath, UK; p20-1
Zenith Halal butchers, Thornton Heath, UK; p20-1
J & J Fish Market, Thornton Heath, UK; p110
Notting Hill carnival; p20-1

Thank you to Tropical Sun/Wanis for contributing dutch pots.

We'd like to also thank those who've supported our social media pages, liked or shared our platform amongst friends and family, or supported us by purchasing this book.

ONLINE REVIEWS

CONNECT WITH US

Follow us @OriginalFlava_

Visit **originalflava.com** to view video recipes.

❤ **@ORIGINALFLAVA_** iewed Original Flava – 5★

You guys are great! Love the recipes, the videos are fun to watch, I can't wait to see more ◆

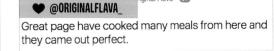

❤ **@ORIGINALFLAVA_**

Great page have cooked many meals from here and they came out perfect.

❤ **@ORIGINALFLAVA_** inal Flava – 5★

Love this page so so happy found this page. Food is on point 😋 Thank you very much you have made me achieve which was once was the impressable.

❤ **@ORIGINALFLAVA_** d Original Flava – 5★

I've made curry goat , rice and peas & also plantain & prawns !! Everything is absolutely delish you need to make a cake or something ◆ satisfy my sweet tooth x

❤ **@ORIGINALFLAVA_** va – 5★

Excellent page. Love all the recipes. Keep up the great work. Also the laughs.

❤ **@ORIGINALFLAVA_** eviewed Original Flava – 5★

The Jerk Salmon with Mango Salsa was absolutely delicious ◆

❤ **@ORIGINALFLAVA_** eviewed Original Flava – 5★

Simple and straightforward to follow. Delicious food made quick and easy.

❤ **@ORIGINALFLAVA_** inal Flava – 5★

Made your saltfish fritters this morning with my son. They tasted amazing for a first attempt. Thankyou! ◆

❤ **@ORIGINALFLAVA_** riginal Flava – 5★

Absolutely love it i love cooking so much and these guys give me many more ideas and little tips i cook the same way good old daddies style ◆◆

❤ **@ORIGINALFLAVA_** d Original Flava – 5★

The recipes are easy to follow and tastes good too!

❤ **@ORIGINALFLAVA_** ved Original Flava – 5★

Your recipes are amazing and produce authentic Caribbean food.

❤ **@ORIGINALFLAVA_** inal Flava – 5★

Love it. I've made the brown stew chicken, escovitch fish and banana fritters. The Jamaican hubby loved every bite!!!